SOLA

SOLA

How the Five Solas Are
Still Reforming the Church

CONTRIBUTORS

Jason K. Allen, GENERAL EDITOR

Jared C. Wilson · Jason G. Duesing

Matthew Barrett · Owen Strachan

MOODY PUBLISHERS

CHICAGO

Interior design: Ragont Design
Cover design: Erik M. Peterson
Cover image of Luther rose copyright © 2010 by ZU_09/iStock (105605744). All rights reserved.

ISBN: 978-0-8024-1873-9

We hope you enjoy this book from Moody Publishers. Our goal is to provide high-quality, thought-provoking books and products that connect truth to your real needs and challenges. For more information on other books and products written and produced from a biblical perspective, go to www.moodypublishers.com or write to:

Moody Publishers
820 N. LaSalle Boulevard
Chicago, IL 60610

1 3 5 7 9 10 8 6 4 2

Printed in the United States of America

With profound appreciation and deep affection,
this book is dedicated to my father- and mother-in-law,
Clayton and Betty Brunson,
who through their steadfast support, helping hands,
constant encouragement, and faithful parenting of my
then-future wife are one of God's greatest blessings in my life.

CONTENTS

FOREWORD

I've had the pleasure of visiting the historic town of Wittenberg, Germany, each of the last two years. Being there on the 500th anniversary of the Protestant Reformation was particularly thrilling. In this little town, Martin Luther (and others) changed the world.

The "motto" of the Reformation was the Latin phrase *post tenebras lux*—that is, "After darkness, light." It was a fitting slogan. The Reformation took place during a spiritually dark time when people were lost in the darkness of corrupt religion, superstition, and idolatry. However, as people heard and read the gospel of *grace alone*, through *faith alone*, in *Christ alone*, many were called out of darkness into God's marvelous light (1 Peter 2:9). God's Word shone in dark places and new believers were called to live all of life in the light of God's truth and grace with *Scripture alone* as their authority and *the glory of God alone* as their aim.

While Luther was a flawed saint, and certainly not the only person responsible for Reformation, I have always been drawn to him for a number of reasons. I have always been moved and challenged by his humble roots, his colorful personality, his disciplined study habits, his radical conversion, his sincere love for his wife, his devotion to the church, his regular practice of hospitality, his deep appreciation of music, his love for children, and his powerful writing and preaching ministry.

I appreciate how Luther utilized the printing press, and his writings remind us of the power of the pen. Luther published a number of small booklets in the common language of the people, and his pamphlets spread across Germany. He also had some artistic help from Lucas Cranach, as noted in Andrew Pettegree's fascinating book, *Brand Luther*. You might think of Cranach as the artist of the Reformation. Cranach not only made portraits of the day's famous Reformers but also made these little gospel pamphlets artistically attractive.

Regarding Luther's preaching, if you ever visit Wittenberg, you will not want to miss St. Mary's Church. St. Mary's is not the church where Luther famously nailed his *Ninety-Five Theses*. It is the other church in town, considered "the mother church of the Reformation." At St. Mary's, Luther preached from 1514 onward, and there you can still see several paintings from Cranach. At the center of the sanctuary, you can see the "Reformation Altarpieces," which are paintings of communion, confession, and other ministries. My favorite is a picture of Luther preaching. It shows Luther with one finger on the text, and the other finger pointing to Christ. And all the people are gazing at the Savior, not their world-famous preacher.

If we are going to see people being led out of darkness into the light today, it will take the same kind of devotion to Christ and His Word. We need millions of faithful ministers that are committed to exalting Jesus from the Scriptures. In a culture that prefers to live according to the rapper Tupac's dark song "All Eyez on Me," we need leaders who will redirect everyone's attention to the light and say, "All eyes on Jesus." The work of evangelism, discipleship, preaching, missions, and church planting all involve centering everything on our all-sufficient Prophet, Priest, and King, Jesus Christ.

I pray that this little book will not only be informative, but also inspiring, as you consider how God used ordinary people during the Reformation to bring about a glorious Christ-centered transformation in churches and in the broader culture. Who's to say the Sovereign Lord will not do something like it again in our dark day? You have some wonderful guides—men who are deeply devoted to the gospel and the church—walking you through the five *solas* to give you such instruction and inspiration.

The historic leaders of the Reformation are gone. They will not preach any more sermons, but living ministers today can preach and teach the five *solas* to a world that remains in darkness. As we face the darkness, let us not shirk back in fear, but let us minster with an unshakable confidence in the gospel of *grace alone* through *faith alone* in *Christ alone*, as testified in *Scripture alone* to *the glory of God alone*.

TONY MERIDA, PhD
Pastor for Preaching and Vision, Imago Dei Church,
Raleigh North Carolina
Author, *The Christ-Centered Expositor*

INTRODUCTION

WHY THE REFORMATION *SOLAS*?
Jason K. Allen

The Protestant Reformation was one of the most pivotal moments in the history of the Christian church. Reflecting on it reminds us that all of life—and especially our spiritual and theological lives—is situated within a historical context. For those who are in Christ, that context is directly influenced by the narrative of the church, what we know as church history.

For evangelicals, remembering and applying the lessons of the Protestant Reformation is of utmost importance. The Reformers are our theological forebears. They fought the good fight; they finished their course; they rediscovered and proclaimed the faith. As evangelicals, we are sons and daughters of the Reformers. And the faith we hold today is summarized beautifully in the five *solas* defended by the Reformers.

WHY FIVE *SOLAS*?

Why five *solas* and from where did they originate?

The five *solas* are the theological distinctives that separated, and do separate, Protestants from the Roman Catholic Church. They are, in a sense, both the cause and the effect, or the precipitating and the resulting convictions, of the Reformation. Though not packaged together in a clear summation of Reformation theology until the twentieth century, each doctrine rose as a theological distinctive worthy of conflict in the sixteenth century.

You might ask, "How can a few Latin clauses be the foundation of a movement the scope of the Protestant Reformation?" Well, in the history of church, short phrases and small words have often caused big divisions necessary for the continued health of the church.

SMALL WORDS, BIG DIVISIONS

Over the past millennia, three major fractures in the church have resulted over three very small words or phrases.

In the eleventh century, the great East and West Schism occurred, separating the Orthodox Church of the East from the Roman Catholic Church of the West. While multiple factors—including competing claims to the papacy—contributed to this divide, the core factor was one Latin word, *filioque*, which describes the Holy Spirit as proceeding from both the Father and the Son.

Post 1517, Protestantism began to fracture into what would become known as denominations. One of the many reasons for this was four Latin words: *hoc est corpus meum*, "This is my body" (see Matt. 26:26; Mark 14:22; Luke 22:19). Disagreement over what Jesus meant when He instituted the Lord's Supper sent Luther, Zwingli, Calvin, and other Reformers in different directions.

The major inflection point, however, the one that we celebrated in 1517 and that continues to separate Protestantism from Roman Catholicism today, is but one word in Latin. The single word that was the driving force of it all was not *fide* (faith) or *gratia* (grace), but first and foremost the word *sola*. Simply meaning "alone," this single word animated Reformers, then and now.

When this one word, "alone," follows the other five Protestant distinctives—*Scripture, faith, grace, Christ,* and *the glory of God*—each carries massive ramifications for theology, for the church, and for your Christian life.

THE FIVE *SOLAS*: AN OVERVIEW

Let's briefly consider the five *solas*, survey their importance, and set the stage for the chapters that follow.

First is *sola Scriptura*. By *sola Scriptura* we mean that "Scripture alone" is the final authority for our lives and for the church. Since God's Word is inspired and true, it is our final and sufficient authority.

Second, there is *sola gratia*, or salvation by "grace alone." We are saved by God's unmerited favor—His goodness shown to us and received by us through faith in Christ's sacrifice. This means that salvation is a monergistic work that God works in our hearts. It is not a synergistic work whereby our good works cooperate with God's efforts. Instead, salvation is, and always has been, by grace alone.

Third is *sola fide*, which means we are justified by "faith alone." We are saved by grace through faith in Christ, not by faith plus works. Faith plus works has never and will never equal salvation. It is through faith that we are justified, and this always results in good works, but our works never procure or merit salvation.

Fourth, there is *solus Christus*, which reminds us that salvation comes to us through "Christ alone." This refers to His sacrificial work, and also to His priestly, mediatorial work. We do not go to a priest today. We celebrate and we thank our pastors, but we are not dependent upon them for a right standing with God.

Fifth and finally is *soli Deo gloria*, which means that salvation is accomplished for "God's glory alone." Our salvation is for His glory. We are the beneficiaries, but He is the one to be praised. As the Old Testament prophets declared, we are saved "for his name's sake."

WHY THE *SOLAS* MATTER

The five *solas* are theological declarations, but they come with massive personal and congregational implications. If the *solas* are true, they provide the doctrinal infrastructure for our spiritual lives. They frame our Christian identities and ministries, and are perennial touchpoints of theological and spiritual formation.

The *solas* are not peripheral matters, positioned to entangle us in needless, tertiary doctrinal squabbles. Rather, they are the essence of the gospel. When we embrace them, we embrace the gospel. When we articulate them, we speak the gospel. When we live consciously of them, we live in the power of the gospel.

Thus, the *solas* establish our Christian life, and they chart it forward. Those who live in light of the five *solas* will experience a more fulfilled and fruitful Christian life. And the church that establishes its ministries on the Reformation *solas* will experience the same.

This book is about just that. In each chapter, I and my friends Jared Wilson, Jason Duesing, Matthew Barrett, and Owen Strachan will introduce you to each of the *solas*. We'll establish them scripturally, situate them within their historical and theological contexts, and then unpack what they mean for your Christian life and church.

Drink deeply from these chapters. As you do, I pray your spiritual life will be informed and invigorated with the gospel of our Lord Jesus Christ.

1

SCRIPTURE ALONE
Jason K. Allen

Sola Scriptura. This truth, that Scripture alone is the sole authority for our beliefs and practices, abides at the center of Reformation theology. It should serve as the believer's guardrails for life, doctrine, and ministry. Scripture alone is to determine what we confess, how we live, and how we order and minister within our churches. For the faithful evangelical, Scripture alone is the authority.

In fact, one can argue that *sola Scriptura* is the most foundational, and the most consequential, of all the *solas. Sola fide* is known as the "material principle." This term means that justification by faith alone is the central truth of the Protestant Reformation. It is the central component of our biblical teaching, and the center of the gospel itself. Yet we call *sola Scriptura* the "formal principle" of the Reformation, because Scripture alone is the singular, authoritative source from which our theology—including *sola fide*—is developed. As the formal principle, *sola Scriptura* is the doctrinal foundation upon which we erect the entirety of Christian belief, including our understanding of the gospel itself.

DEFINING *SOLA SCRIPTURA*

For the Reformers specifically, Scripture alone meant the Bible held authority over all church tradition, popes, and councils. The point was not that tradition, popes, or councils could not instruct the church. Rather, it was that all these were subordinate to, and thus subject to, the Word of God. In other words, the Word of God regulates them; they don't regulate the Word of God.

In our day, we as evangelicals also confirm that Scripture alone holds authority over popes, councils, and traditions. Yet, we should add to that list experience, preference, and pragmatic considerations. For Luther—and for us— Scripture is the *norma normans*, the determining norm by which everything else is measured. It is the standard, the benchmark, the plumb line for the church.

Sola Scriptura means that Scripture establishes the church; the church does not establish the Scriptures. Scripture judges the church; the church does not judge the Scriptures. The church did not create the Scriptures; the Scriptures created the church. As Luther argued, "Who begets his own parent? Who first brings forth his own maker?"[1]

MORE THAN AN ABSTRACT DOCTRINE

But Scripture alone is more than an abstract doctrine. Reflective Christians realize the singular role Scripture has played in their own spiritual formation. My conversion was rooted in the preaching of the gospel and the Word of God. And so was yours.

James teaches us we were born again "by the word of truth" (James 1:18). Peter reminds us,

> For you have been born again not of seed which is perishable but imperishable, that is, through the living and enduring word of God. For,
>
> "All flesh is like grass,
> And all its glory like the flower of grass.
> The grass withers,
> And the flower falls off,
> But the word of the Lord endures forever."
>
> And this is the word which was preached to you.
> (1 Peter 1:23–26 NASB)

God also used His Word to call me into the ministry. God gripped my heart with Romans 10 and the Pastoral Epistles. As I studied the Scriptures, my call to ministry was clarified and intensified. The Scriptures seemed to demand that I preach them.

That's true of all who are called into the ministry. A call to the ministry is a call to minister the Word.[2]

Sola Scriptura also framed my theological convictions, including my denominational commitment. I continuously look to the Scriptures to determine what I am to believe and how the church is to be ordered. Even though I was reared in a Baptist home, my Baptist convictions were confirmed and strengthened after a thorough study of Scripture. This is how it was for me, and how it should be for you. The effects of *sola Scriptura* extend to all aspects of our lives. It is the authority for all we do.

Sola Scriptura is an eminently practical doctrine, determining far more about us spiritually, ministerially, and theologically than we may realize. My goal in this chapter is for you to consider *sola Scriptura*'s expansiveness. This will be accomplished in three ways. First, we will establish *sola Scriptura* biblically. Second, we will contextualize it historically in the sixteenth century. And third, we will apply it pastorally.

ESTABLISHING *SOLA SCRIPTURA* BIBLICALLY

Within the Bible, the doctrine of *sola Scriptura* is most clearly seen in 2 Timothy 3:15–17. Paul, in his final letter to his son in ministry, Timothy, charges him to stand strong in the gospel and to be faithful in his ministry. Paul exhorts him to stand firm and to preach the Word.

Timothy, we know, is vacillating. He is discouraged. He is weakened. Many have abandoned him in the faith. So Paul, beginning in chapter three, documents the effects of sin and all that is going wrong in the church. He then charges Timothy to remain strong. Paul reminds Timothy in verse 12 that "all who desire to live godly in Christ Jesus will be persecuted" (NASB). In verses 14–15, he continues, "You, however," as opposed to those who have forsaken the faith, "continue in the things you have learned and become convinced of, knowing from whom you have learned them, and that from childhood you have learned the sacred writings which are able to give you the wisdom that leads to salvation through faith which is in Christ Jesus" (NASB).

Paul is reminding Timothy that he was taught the truth of the Scriptures from his mother and his grandmother at an early age. He is reminding Timothy that as he was taught the Old Testament, a new way of life came to him through the Scriptures. Here, Paul is saying the Old Testament makes the gospel clear. It makes faith in the coming Messiah clear.

Then, in verses 16–17, Paul writes this great passage that so much of the doctrine of Scripture is built upon. This verse should be interpreted with an anticipatory sense, meaning Paul is also foreshadowing the rest of coming revelation and the closure of the cannon. He says this: "All Scripture is inspired by God and profitable for teaching, for reproof, for correction, for training in righteousness; so that the man of God may be adequate, equipped for every good work" (NASB).

The first part of verse 16, "all Scripture is inspired" is significant. This word "inspired," which in Greek is *theopneustos*, means "having been breathed out from God's innermost being." Also, notice that Paul says, "*all* Scripture." It is not up to us, or to the critic, to pick and choose what portion of Scripture we deem to be from God and thus true. Moreover, it is not left to us to pick and choose which portions of Scripture we think are most applicable or most urgently needing to be obeyed.

What Paul states here in seed form is the verbal, plenary inspiration of Scripture. All of Scripture, not some of it, is inspired. The words themselves are inspired, not just the thoughts of the authors or the intent of the authors, but every last word. *All* Scripture is inspired by God.

Often, I will hear this verse read, and it will be insinuated that there is a period placed after the word "God": "All Scripture is inspired by God." But notice Paul takes it further than that: "All Scripture is inspired by God *and* is profitable for teaching and for reproof" (emphasis added). The Scriptures teach us many things, but specifically what to believe. They convict and reprove us by correcting our errant beliefs. This correction then trains us in righteousness. In other words, Scripture has a direct effect on how we live.

Verse 17 continues, "so that the man of God may be adequate, equipped for every good work." Paul is basically saying, "Timothy, as you minister, as you preach, as you live, know this: Your weapon in the kingdom is the Word of God. Your tool is the Word of God. And as you wield it faithfully, you will be equipped for every good work." So, we don't have to search to and fro, looking for a mystical experience, some kind of charismatic reception of gifts, or something to make us complete and worthy to minister. Verse 17 teaches that by the Spirit of God, and with the Word of God, we have been made ready to minister.

The logic here is clear, is it not? If this Word is of God, then it must of necessity be true. And if it is of God and true, it must be authoritative. Thus, we are called to submit our lives to it.

Thus, *sola Scriptura*, biblically speaking, is the acknowledgement that Scripture enjoys a singular status as God's Word. Therefore, it is the believer's final, ultimate authority.

SOLA SCRIPTURA HISTORICALLY

Now that we have established *sola Scriptura* biblically, let's contextualize it historically. The doctrine is displayed in a man: Martin Luther. Journey with me back to the sixteenth century, to the years 1517, 1519, and 1521. What took place in Luther's mind and heart during that era, and the convictions he came to, illumine *sola Scriptura* for us.

First, we should acknowledge that the five *solas* were not packaged together in the sixteenth century as we know them now. They were present then, but as far as being packaged together, that was an early twentieth century phenomenon as the legacy of Protestantism was further crystalized.

For Luther, though, we don't see him sending out *sola Scriptura* public service announcements. Rather, he grew into this conviction over a period of years. He reasoned within himself through a number of conflicts. So, to understand this doctrine historically, it is best to look at it through the prism of Luther and three pivotal scenes in church history. Two of these scenes are familiar to many of us, but one is not.

The first scene is Reformation Day, October 31, 1517. Luther, the young Augustinian monk, nailed his *Ninety-five Theses* to the door of the Wittenberg Castle Church. He was concerned about many issues, but at the heart of it all was the selling of indulgences. This is perhaps the most dastardly abuse of authority in the church's history. In response, Luther set forth these ninety-five theses for discussion. He was not initially seeking to leave the Roman Church but to strengthen it. He intended to spark a debate. Instead, he sparked a conflagration that would sweep throughout Europe and beyond.

The second scene occurred in the spring of 1521. It is less familiar than the posting of the *Ninety-five Theses* but still relatively well-known. The Diet of Worms—which was convened by Charles V, emperor of the Holy Roman Empire—took place just four years after Luther had posted his theses.

The Emperor called Luther to give an account for what he had said and written. Luther was granted assurance of safe travel and promised that he would not be put to death upon arrival. He showed up April 16, at 4:00 p.m., and was told to report the next day at the same time. He entered the assembly and took his place in the middle of the auditorium. Before him were his collected writings and around him a gathering of ecclesiastical and imperial authorities. At this point for Luther, his choice was binary: reaffirm his writings or renounce them.

In reading the account, you can almost feel the weight and

drama of the moment. The presiding officer, Johann Eck, asked Luther if the collected books were his and if he was prepared to retract their heresies. Luther asked for twenty-four hours to pray and deliberate.

The gathering reconvened on April 18 at 4:00 p.m. There, Luther declared the words that are written in immortal ink:

> Unless I am convinced by the testimony of the Scriptures or by clear reason (for I do not trust either in the pope or in councils alone, since it is well known that they have often erred and contradicted themselves), I am bound by the Scriptures I have quoted and my conscience is captive to the Word of God. I cannot and I will not recant anything, since it is neither safe nor right to go against conscience. I cannot do otherwise, here I stand, may God help me, Amen.[3]

In other words, Luther articulated the doctrine of *sola Scriptura*.

Finally, and the most pivotal of the three scenes as it relates to *sola Scriptura*, is sandwiched between the two previous accounts and is often the one most overlooked. This third event was the Leipzig Debate of 1519.

On previous occasions, Luther affirmed Holy Scripture as completely authoritative, but as he gathered at the Leipzig Debate, this concept was clarified within him. Luther was called to debate Johann Eck, the German scholastic theologian who would later preside at the Diet of Worms. Here is where, it appears, he almost stumbled into the doctrine of *sola Scriptura*. Eck was formidable, yet Luther held him with antipathy, as he did most all his critics. Luther declared Eck to be a "little glory-hungry beast."[4]

In the debate, Luther was the better exegete, but Eck was the better historian. Eck's strategy was to link Luther to his forbearer, Jan Hus. The church had officially condemned Hus and his teaching, so Eck knew if he linked Luther to Hus, Luther would thus bring on his own condemnation.

Eck pressed Luther to affirm Hus, who a century earlier at the Council of Constance, was burned at the stake. Luther, perhaps, would meet the same fate. However, a funny thing happened at Leipzig. During the fracas, they took a lunch break where Luther slipped out and reread the reports from the Council of Constance—reminding himself of what took place and reminding himself of what Hus claimed.

The debate resumed, and Luther declared, "I am a Hussite." He knew exactly what he was saying. He knew precisely what was taking place. And in that moment, he was in essence saying, "I stand with Hus. We are men of the Book."

Hus made a prophesy before he was martyred, saying, "Today you burn a goose, but in one hundred years a swan will arise which you will prove unable to boil or roast."[5] Luther received that mantle and perceived Hus to be prophesying about him. This is why today in Lutheran churches the pulpit will often be in the shape of a swan.

At Leipzig, Eck's whole plan was to back Luther into a corner by pressing him to affirm Hus. Luther was backing Eck, and all who were present, into a corner by saying, in effect, "Your popes have failed. Your councils have failed. In fact, they have contradicted one another. So, if you do not have a pope who is legitimately authoritative, and you do not have a council that is authoritative, then what do you have?" Luther stood on *sola Scriptura*.

SOLA SCRIPTURA AND YOUR CHURCH

Now that we have established *sola Scriptura* biblically and historically, let's apply it pastorally. The demand of *sola Scriptura* is that we are obliged to submit our lives to the Word of God. As we do, we experience a more satisfied and fruitful Christian life, and most of all, we glorify God. Thus, here are ten words of application for you, your Christian ministry, and your church.

First, any belief in *sola Scriptura* worth standing on necessitates a pulpit ministry that preaches the Word. Why we preach, when we preach, and how we preach all reveal what we believe about the Word of God. If we confess to believe the Book but do not preach it, then we are merely running our mouths. But if we believe that the Bible is God's true Word, God's authoritative Word, and God's sufficient Word, then we must be intentional about bringing it to bear on our lives and the lives of others. It should affect the whole of our ministries, most especially our pulpit ministries.

Second, it shapes our soul care and how well pastors shepherd the flock of God. At the end of the day, we want to bring the Word of God to bear with grace—prayerfully applying it to other people's lives. This is not just something that magically happens, though, we must be intentional about it. It is also not merely done from the pulpit, but from across the coffee table, in small group settings, and in the study where people come for counsel. We must bring the Word to bear in every aspect of our ministries. Ministers are often expected to be wonder workers, able to speak helpful words, magically improving the lives of our hearers. We can't do that, but God's Word can. We must simply unleash it, so it can work in the lives of people.

Third, this doctrine should lead us to strive for church unity. Luther was right on many things, but he can be faulted for being naïve about one thing. He assumed that a return to Scriptural authority and casting off the conflicting shackles of popes and councils would facilitate a new wave of mission fervor and church unity. The Reformation certainly brought fervor, but it did not quite bring unity. To be frank, today there is too much fragmentation in the church of the Lord Jesus Christ. I am not suggesting that we water down doctrine, but I am suggesting that as we preach and stand on *sola Scriptura*, we do so in a way that fosters unity in the body of Christ. As we do, we should be intentional about seeking to do so with like-minded brothers and sisters of strong evangelical faith. It is essential that we strive for unity.

Fourth, this doctrine calls for faithful, disciplined biblical interpretation. Interpretation matters. If you're going to say you are committed to the Bible, and that it is true, then how you interpret it makes all the difference. Be diligent and be devoted to the study of God's Word. Learn to properly employ the tools needed to rightly interpret the Bible. This Book is not an open sesame for us to read into it what we want. This book is God's Word, and it requires us to faithfully and humbly interpret it.

Fifth, a commitment to *sola Scriptura* brings with it, I believe, a commitment to confessional statements. Why? Because it quickly turns into a slippery slope when people say, "We just believe the book. We have no creed but the Bible." This is a place you do not want to go. My denomination articulates its beliefs via the *Baptist Faith and Message 2000*. We also confess our beliefs from the *Danvers Statement on Biblical Manhood and Womanhood* as well as the *Chicago Statement on Biblical Inerrancy*. We are a confessional people and we do not let *sola Scriptura* sleepwalk us into nonsensical statements like, "We confess no creed but the Bible." To confess that is to confess no creed at all. While the doctrine of *sola Scriptura* teaches us that Scripture alone is the final authority for our beliefs and practices, we need confessions and statements to help us better understand what Scripture teaches.

Sixth, we must have a strong commitment to regenerate church membership. As evangelicals, we do not have a pope, and we do not want one. We do not have councils either. We have the local church and the Word of God. The local church gathered is where God's people come together and humbly seek God's will for the church under the leadership of its pastors. If we have a Book that is true, and people of God who are in submission to it, then the last thing we need is a pope. Rather, a firm commitment to regenerate church membership guarantees that when the local church is gathered, they are united under the banner of the Word of God.

Seventh, a commitment to *sola Scriptura* is a commitment to Christ-centered theology. When we look to the Scriptures we look to Jesus, and any firm grasp of *sola Scriptura* leads to the necessity of a deeper commitment to the preaching of Christ. We are called to bring the Savior to bear, to proclaim the Lord Jesus Christ so that sinners will hear and believe; so that repentance will take place in the hearts of people; so that boys and girls, men and women would be saved; so that the Great Commission would be proclaimed. That is what we do.

Eighth, *sola Scriptura* leads to a ministry that is marked by gravity and perspective. Imagine Luther before the world's authorities, eking out the words, "Here I stand." Imagine Luther in 1517 strolling toward the door of the Castle Church and nailing these theses on the door, knowing what would likely happen. Imagine Luther at Leipzig during that lunch break, reminding himself of the Council of Constance and realizing, *I believe this. I believe this. I believe this.* He knew fully the consequences when he walked back out and said, "I am a Hussite." This historical context puts in perspective so many of our present concerns, which, in light of global Christianity and church history, are superficial. This ought to infuse our ministries with a sense of gratitude, knowing that there are many previous believers who paid the ultimate price that they could pay for the faith we received: their lives.

Ninth, *sola Scriptura* shapes our worship. For many Protestants, and for me personally, *sola Scriptura* means a commitment to the regulative principle for corporate worship on the Lord's Day. Simply stated, the regulative principle argues that our worship should include those elements specifically called for in the New Testament, including the public reading of Scripture, the preaching of the Word, the singing of psalms, hymns, and spiritual songs, and, of course, baptism and the Lord's Supper. We are to preach the Scriptures, read the Scriptures, pray the Scriptures, and sing the Scriptures. The doctrine of *sola Scriptura* affects everything, especially how we think about and structure our weekly gathering for worship.

Tenth and finally, *sola Scriptura* encourages us to put the "protest" back into Protestantism. What are the great challenges of our generation? What is God calling you or your ministry to stand for? You may not know the answer today. You may stumble into it eight years from now in your local church gathering. You might be pressed into your own little crucible when you decline to marry a leading church benefactor's daughter because she is living in sin. You might find yourself in conflict when you are willing to stand on the Word of God and speak to issues of sexuality and gender. The society pressures us to be silent. As with every generation before, our task is to take the baton of faith, the truth that we have received, and to be faithful to pass it on to the next.

Sola Scriptura is more than an abstract doctrine; it is a truth that is essential for our Christian lives and our local church ministries. *Sola Scriptura* indeed is the formal principle of the Reformation—and it is to be the formal principle of our lives. As Luther discovered, everything else rests upon it. Have you discovered the same?

2

GRACE ALONE
Jared C. Wilson

---

*Contrariwise, the world cannot suffer those things to be
condemned which it most esteemeth, and best liketh of;
and therefore it chargeth the gospel that it is a sedi-
tious doctrine, and full of errors; that it overthroweth
commonwealths, countries, dominions, kingdoms, and
empires, and therefore offendeth both against God and
the emperor; abolisheth laws, corrupteth good man-
ners, and setteth all men at liberty to do what they list.
Wherefore, with just zeal, and high service to God, (as
it would seem) it persecuteth this doctrine, and abhor-
reth the teachers and professors thereof, as the greatest
plague that can be in the whole earth.[1]*

Thus, the Reformer Martin Luther writes in his opening commentary on chapter 1, verse 1 of Paul's letter to the Galatians. This work of Luther's still remains one of the crown jewels in his immense body of theological and exegetical work, its power belied by its apparent simplicity. In that way, it is like the gospel itself.

What was the Reformation, really? What Luther and the Reformers undertook was nothing less than *a recovery movement*. They were retrieving from the deep, dank basement of the church the pure, potent, dangerous message of free grace in Christ. In the excerpt above, Luther touches on just how toxic to self-righteousness and religious pride this message really is, and why it was locked up for so long, obscured and suppressed.

The self-justifying cannot abide the gospel. It is a rogue element in their tidy moralistic world. And anyone who comes along preaching its true form is treated, as Luther says, as one who has the plague. "Don't stand too close to that gospel guy. He's contagious."

The hallmark of the Reformation theology that Protestants cherish today is, of course, the doctrine of *sola fide*—justification by faith alone. But at the heart of faith alone must pulse the blood of *sola gratia*, the notion that our justification—indeed, the whole of our salvation—rests ultimately and solely on the grace of God given in Christ.

But "grace alone" is not simply a notion, an idea. Because Reformational theology *as an idea* saves nobody. No, the grace alone of Christ alone, I believe, is the heart of Christianity. I think this is the case Paul is making in the entirety of his letter to the Galatians, and I want to share some Reformational thoughts with you on *sola gratia* reflected in chapter 3, verses 19–26. Paul writes,

> Why then was the law given? It was added for the sake of transgressions until the Seed to whom the promise was made would come. The law was put into effect through angels by means of a mediator. Now a mediator is not just for one person alone, but God is one. Is the law therefore contrary to God's promises? Absolutely not! For if the law had been granted with the ability to give life, then righteousness would certainly be on the basis of the law. But the Scripture imprisoned everything under sin's power, so that the promise might be given on the basis of faith in Jesus Christ to those who believe. Before this faith came, we were confined under the law, imprisoned until the coming faith was revealed. The law, then, was our guardian until Christ, so that we could be justified by faith. But since that faith has come, we are no longer under a guardian, for through faith you are all sons of God in Christ Jesus. (CSB)

Biblical Christianity hinges on where you put the "yes-but" in the gospel presentation. Our impulse, just as it was for the corrupted church of Luther's day, is to *yes-but* grace. Something wells up inside of us, our flesh bristles at the notion of grace, and we begin thinking of all that could go wrong if someone "really took it too far." And so we barge into the counseling room of someone's heart with all of our religious caveats and legal enhancements. Our fear is that the gospel will not hold, that grace cannot do the work. We want to shore it up with good works.

This is what is going on in Galatia. This is what drives Paul to such passionate lengths to stress the centrality of the gospel. The Judaizers have come along to *yes-but* the gospel: "Oh, sure, sure, salvation is by grace, but you really need to get circumcised and practice the ceremonial law if you want to be saved."

Beware of the "plus" that anxious people constantly try to add to Jesus. Because grace is the heart of Christianity. And grace alone is the basis of our salvation. As Kevin Vanhoozer says, "*Sola gratia* is a permanent reminder that at the heart of Christianity is good news."[2]

Luther famously declared that *sola fide* is the article upon which the church stands or falls. With all the cheeky presumption the gospel may provoke, I would suggest we add that *sola gratia* is the article upon which *sola fide* stands or falls. "Grace alone," in fact, is the heart of the other four *solas*, the throughline or, if you like, the "decoder ring" to the rest.

I think we even see this dynamic relationship represented in Galatians 3. For instance, Paul's view of Scripture, even as he writes it, is intrinsically and explicitly grace-reliant. It is a grace that we even have the Scriptures, and the Scriptures mediate the grace of Christ the Mediator to us. This is why Paul begins every one of his letters with some form of the phrase "grace to you" and concludes with some form of the phrase "grace with you." He is recognizing, in the very composition, that God's breathed-out words are a grace and deliver a grace, that to embrace a Spirit-inspired letter is to be, in some form, receiving grace. Connecting the doctrine of special revelation to the doctrine of grace, then, we may say that:

GRACE ALONE IS THE THEME OF SCRIPTURE ALONE

Sola Scriptura can be only because of *sola gratia*. This can be a difficult point to understand, and so many get it wrong, because so much biblical ink is spilled on the law, on the imperatives, especially in the old covenant Scriptures. This is why, in many parts of evangelicalism, the mistaken notion persists that the patriarchs were saved by their works, not by their faith. For my part, I didn't understand that grace alone is the through-line of the Bible's presentation of salvation, cover to cover, until I was an adult. The narratives before Christ certainly *seem* weighted to the law. But there is a reason for that—and it isn't so we'd think of salvation as being mediated through our obedience. This is what Paul writes in Galatians 3:22, "But the Scripture imprisoned everything under sin's power, so that the promise might be given on the basis of faith in Jesus Christ to those who believe" (CSB).

The Bible gives us both the diagnosis for our condition *and* the antidote. But we will misunderstand the antidote if we misunderstand the diagnosis. This is why, to put it plainly, legalism is just so stupid. Legalism imagines that the solution to your problem (inadequate righteousness) is more of your problem.

The legalistic Christian purports to make much of the law but in fact does an injustice to the law of God because he makes the law out to be something manageable!

To understand the gospel in the context of the Scriptures means understanding how the law functions in the "salvation equation." Obedience must come as a result of justification, as a response to the justifying work of God in Christ. It does not precipitate or contribute to justification in any way. What the law does when it is first introduced is present the problem and prepare the heart for the sweetness of the gospel. The power of the law isn't freedom; it is death. Therefore, to "package" the gospel of justification with legal remedies is to disorder the gospel proclamation. The Galatian Judaizers—teachers who were insisting that Gentile converts to Christianity must adhere to the Jewish dietary and ceremonial laws—were perpetrators of this disorder.

But there is also an opposite danger at work in some corners of the so-called gospel-centered movement. It is perhaps not as great a danger as the legalistic impulse, but it is a danger nonetheless. There is an implicit antinomianism[3] at work in many Christian hearts and in some Christian circles.

We must be mindful of how centering grace can be. It can keep us out of the ditch of legalism on the one side and out of the ditch of antinomianism on the other. Remember, to be gospel-centered is not to be law-neglecting or law-flippant.

How can we be flippant about what reveals the holiness of

God? To be flippant about the law is to be flippant about God.

How can we be flippant about what David delighted in? To be flippant about the law is to be flippant about worship.

How can we be flippant about what Christ took seriously enough to fulfill? To be flippant about the law is to be flippant about Christ (and His sacrifice).

How can we be flippant about what Paul has taken great pains to declare as righteous, spilling much ink by the inspiration of the Spirit? To be flippant about the law is to be flippant about the word of the Spirit.

Make no mistake: the law cannot do what the gospel does. But the law is not bad. It is good. It is good at accomplishing what it is designed to do.

Two years ago, I almost died in Australia. It is actually not that hard to die in Australia, so it's extremely easy to *almost* die. My wife, Becky, and I were taken by our host to a beach just north along the coast of Sydney. We enjoyed walking on the sand and listening to the waves, but our favorite thing to do was to venture out onto the rocky outcroppings into the ocean. There was a series of rocky ledges, long and flat, multiple plateaus at different levels, each riddled with little streams and dotted with pretty, little tide pools. We were just strolling around, navigating the crevices, picking up anemones and starfish, watching tiny fish dart around.

At the end of the ledge, the rocks abruptly dropped into the ocean, which was splashing up foamy spray over the edge. We wandered up near the edge of the outcropping, feeling the mist in the air and watching the powerful waves crash against the rock beneath us. We had spent nearly thirty minutes exploring this area, so we felt no real sense of danger. No wave had crested the ledge, so we assumed we were fine. And then it happened. A rogue wave came crashing up over the edge of the cliff and knocked Becky and me over. I fell backwards into a crevice and was covered in water. I began to panic. All I could think about was the water being drawn back out and the prospect of us being dragged with it, sucked out to sea.

We frantically made our way back over cracks and pools we couldn't see because of the water level now and eventually made it to shore. I was panting, scared, and my legs were covered in blood from all the falls and scrapes.

What happened? I had been prancing about on those rocks like a king in his natural castle, careless and carefree. I was king of the world. Until the wave put me in my place.

The word of the law is like that. We are minding our business, kings of the world, lords of our own lives, and then we are confronted by the reality of God and it stops us, silences us, wrecks our sense of self-sufficiency. It quiets us, stifles us. As Paul writes in Romans 3:19, "We know that whatever the law says it speaks to those who are under the law, so that every mouth may be stopped."

This is what Paul is recalling in Galatians 3 when he says that Scripture is imprisoning everything under sin's power. And yet there's something else the Scripture is doing with the law. In light of the gospel, the law is put in its place. Thus, verse 24: "The law, then, was our guardian until Christ, so that we could be justified by faith."

The commandments and their application are our guardian, our "tutor," training us to yearn for Christ, making us long for the remedy of Christ, for the remedy of His grace. The same law that shows us God's holiness reveals our utter unholiness, so properly understanding this prison we're in makes us long for liberation.

But the Bible is such a heavenly book, it puts the key to our cell inside the cell itself! So from beginning to end, we see in these Scriptures that God's disposition toward His people is one of grace. By delaying the due date of death of Adam and Eve, covering their shame with animal skins. By meeting with Abraham, using Moses, stewarding the people's sinful demand for a king to bring about the lineage of the Messiah, in multiple ways throughout multiple centuries, all along, the same pages that would seem to lend themselves to the highlight of works are whispering "grace, grace, grace." This is the point of Galatians 3:8, and it's the whole point of Hebrews 11, and this is why Jesus says what He does to those disciples on the road to Emmaus (Luke 24:27).

Now, you may say, "I understand that grace is the theme of Scripture, but how does grace alone fit with the idea of Scripture alone?"

Here is how: When you deny the ultimate authority of Scripture, for instance, it is because you are erecting other ultimate authorities in your life—historically speaking, for the Reformation era, the Roman Church or the papacy. And the

Roman Church and the papacy do not represent a protection of salvation by grace but *an addition*. You diminish the ultimacy of Scripture's authority, you engage in legalism, by adding other authorities to the divine authority of the Word. When you *yes-but* the Word of God, you inevitably *yes-but* the gospel.

This is why in many churches every Sunday where the authority of Scripture is nodded to, but the sufficiency of Scripture is not practiced, you inevitably receive a message dominated by imperatives ("things to do"). The idea is that the proclamation of the biblical gospel is insufficient for transformation, that we must add to it with our works. And while good works are non-negotiable in the Christian life, of course, when we prioritize imperatives over indicatives, we implicitly undermine the sufficiency of the gospel to change people. These churches tend to *yes-but* "Scripture alone" and in effect *yes-but* "grace alone." When you begin to compromise the sufficiency of Scripture, you compromise the sufficiency of grace.

Secondly, however, the tenet of *sola gratia* gives the tenet of *sola fide* its substance, connecting grace to another level in the Reformational treasure. We might put it this way:

GRACE ALONE IS THE STRENGTH OF FAITH ALONE

What exactly *is* faith? One of the problems people often have with understanding the Protestant doctrine of *sola fide* arises from the difficulty of defining *faith* without speaking to works.

James is of course right—faith without works is dead (James 2:17, 26). Faith without works isn't even faith. That is how connected and inextricably tangled they are.

When I was a teenager, I traveled with our church youth choir once to perform a musical in different churches. At the end of each performance, our youth pastor would come out on stage and deliver a gospel presentation. Every night, he included the same illustration about faith. "Imagine," he said, "a crowd gathered at the Grand Canyon to watch a man walking across the deep gorge on a tightrope. He brings out a wheelbarrow and asks the crowd, 'How many of you think I can push this wheelbarrow across the gap?' Nearly everyone raises their hand. So, the man performs the trick, walking the empty wheelbarrow across and back. 'Now,' he says, 'who thinks I can do the same trick with someone inside the wheelbarrow?' Many hands once again go up. 'Okay,' he says, 'who would like to get in the wheelbarrow?' Nobody volunteered."

This was the illustration of true faith. You can say you believe the wheelbarrow will hold you, that the man is skilled enough to get you there and back across the deadly gap, but you don't *really* trust if you aren't willing to get in.

I thought about this and thought about this, and I still have trouble untangling it in my mind. How can faith alone consist of works? Getting in the wheelbarrow is a work, is it not? It is a work sprung from faith, to be sure, but it's a work nonetheless.

We struggle, then, to slice between faith and works, as we hold to this idea of faith alone doing the justifying. We can't separate them, but we have to distinguish them. How do you define faith? Answer: belief. Well, what is belief? Answer: trust. Well, what is trust? The thinner we slice it, the more remains.

The Bible talks a lot about faith in a variety of ways, of course, but we are offered really only one definition. It is found in Hebrews 11:1, which reads, "Now faith is the assurance of things hoped for, the conviction of things not seen."

Faith is an assurance of something not yet received and conviction about something which, at the moment, is invisible. This is why Paul uses the word "promise" throughout his letter to the Romans and why he uses it here in Galatians 3:21.

The patriarchs believed in "the promise." How does this relate to faith? I think it may be helpful to think of faith alone, apart from works, as a kind of emptiness. An empty hand, so to speak, or, as John Calvin put it, "a kind of vessel."[4] We must believe in justification by faith alone because only God can justify us and only faith is a vehicle "empty" enough to rest on the infinitude of God. Faith is a disposition of weakness. It must have an object. (As Calvin goes on to say, "Faith of itself does not possess the power of justifying, but only in so far as it receives Christ."[5]) The object of faith may not be God, of course, but faith doesn't exist where it doesn't exist "in" something. You can have faith in religion, faith in your family, faith in yourself, but you can't simply "have faith."

I recall a woman I once pastored referring to her own need to "trust in her faith." I gently suggested this was inadvisable, if only because it is nonsensical. You don't put trust in your trust or faith in your faith. This is like saying I grasp hold of my grasp.

I know defining faith this way sounds strange since *sola fide* is, according to Luther, the article upon which the church is said to stand or fall. I'm essentially arguing that the article upon which the whole church stands or falls is the one about weakness. I think this is entirely acceptable, given the spiritual economy of the gospel. Grace brings the strength. Faith brings the weakness. And this is the essence of Christianity, what Luther frequently referred to as the "wonderful exchange" of our sin for Christ's righteousness.

We are saved by grace through faith, and it's not of ourselves (Eph. 2:8). You come to that bargaining table with all the world of treasures in your hand, and you will cheapen the righteousness of Christ. He says, "Come and bring your emptiness. Bring your nothingness. Bring your poverty of spirit, and I will give you *everything*." But if you bring one penny, the deal is off.

We are justified by faith alone, but that faith must be in something. Therefore, our justification is on the basis of faith alone, but our faith is on the basis of grace alone.

Again, notice what Paul writes in Galatians 3:21: "Is the law therefore contrary to God's promises? Absolutely not! For if the law had been granted with the ability to give life, then righteousness would certainly be on the basis of the law" (CSB).

Faith is the basis of justification, but what is the basis of faith? Not the law!

Yes, faith without works is dead. Yes, our works are the corroborating evidence of our faith. And indeed the grace that faith lays hold of empowers our works. But when you start entering the world of technicalities and soteriological minutiae, talking about "initial justification" versus "final salvation" and so on and so forth, you can cause confusion over issues that ought to be clear as day for sinners in need of a Savior. The gospel is more powerful than any other force under heaven, but it isn't rocket science.

The matters of salvation can be complex and good fodder for theologians, but let me just encourage you thusly: Don't get too smart for the good news! The gospel is big, glorious, and multi-faceted. But be careful making it complicated. If you complicate the gospel, you can complicate people right out of the kingdom, which is exactly what the Judaizers did. What is your faith resting on? It must be grace, or your faith is sunk. Grace brings the strength to the weakness of faith. Grace empowers God's people (Acts 6:8), animates our obedience (1 Cor. 15:10), fuels our worship (2 Cor. 4:15), sustains us in suffering (2 Cor. 12:9), trains us to renounce unrighteousness (Titus 2:11–12), dispenses mercy in our times of need (Heb. 4:16), and strengthens our hearts (Heb. 13:9). "God is able," Paul writes in 2 Corinthians 9:8, "to make all grace abound to you, so that having all sufficiency in all things at all times, you may abound in every good work."

Even your faith, Ephesians 2:8 reminds us, is a gift from God. Even your faith is birthed by grace (Acts 18:27; Rom. 1:5). Salvation is all of grace. It's not turtles all the way down, it's grace!

As Gresham Machen says, "Christ will do everything, or nothing, and the only hope is to throw ourselves unreservedly on His mercy and trust Him for all."[6]

Grace alone is the strength of faith alone. How much hope

would you have otherwise? When your faith is struggling, weak, frail, battered—how is it that it might still sustain you, might still move mountains even?

The law has not been granted the ability to give life, Paul tells us (Gal. 3:21). Through faith, you are not employees of God, but sons (3:26).

Look, when you're alone and despondent, sitting at that dining room table in the wee hours of the night, head in your hands, wondering how you will make it through, overburdened and overwhelmed, feeling lost and rejected and ashamed and anxious, and Jesus Christ walks through that door to stand under the kitchen light with you—what kind of look do you think is on His face? This makes all the difference in the world. The strength of faith alone is grace alone.

Thirdly, however, we must note how this grace is not some ethereal virtue, some spiritual "good feelings" sent our way from "the man upstairs." No, grace is given incarnate. Thus:

GRACE ALONE IS FOUND IN CHRIST ALONE

If you go anywhere else but Christ, you will not find grace, but only more legal demands for righteousness. This is why "grace alone" is crucial to understanding "Christ alone": because it's possible to have faith in a Christ alone who is not the real Christ.

When you're weary and worn out at that kitchen table, when you're stumbling home awash in shame from going too far physically with your boyfriend or girlfriend, when you're look-ing at that computer screen tempted to look at pornography or swimming in guilt because you just did—*who is Christ to you?*

What is on the face of the Savior? Do you see the disap-pointed taskmaster? Or do you see grace alone?

Paul writes in Romans 2:4 that it is God's kindness that leads us to repentance and in Titus 2:11–12 that it is grace that trains us to renounce unrighteousness.

We can expect the holy Lord may discipline us. There may be serious consequences for our sin in this life. But in Christ: There. Is. No. Condemnation (Rom. 8:1). If you're a minister, especially, and you don't believe Christ approaches sinners awash in guilt and shame with a disposition of grace, let me advise you to find another profession.

The law comes prancing about, strutting its stuff. And the voice of the accuser knows how to use it. "Look at this area of your life," "Look at this corner of your heart," "You could never have the blessings of God," "How in the world could God love you?" The legal demands are just doing their thing, sizing you up, announcing your deficit of glory, condemning, shaming. *And then the rogue wave of the gospel comes* and shuts it up.

The apostle writes in Galatians 3:22, "But the Scripture im-prisoned everything under sin's power, so that the promise might be given on the basis of *faith in Jesus Christ* to those who believe" (CSB, emphasis added).

And in verse 24: "The law was our guardian *until Christ*" (ESV, emphasis added).

And in verse 26: "for through faith you are all sons of God *in Christ Jesus*" (CSB, emphasis added).

It is crucial where you put the *yes-but* in Christianity. Don't *yes-but* the gospel with the law; *yes-but* the law with the gospel.

Luther in his commentary warns us,

> The Law is not to operate on a person after he has been humbled and frightened by the exposure of his sins and the wrath of God. We must then say to the Law: "Mister Law, lay off him. He has had enough. You scared him good and proper." Now it is the Gospel's turn. Now let Christ with His gracious lips talk to him of better things, grace, peace, forgiveness of sins, and eternal life.[7]

For Luther, grace is not a disembodied virtue. We're not condemned by the holiness of God only to be redeemed by some amorphous "good vibe" called grace. Grace must be mediated (Gal. 3:20), just like the law was mediated.

And what better mediator of grace than He who perfectly fulfills the law? In this way, the grace mediated to us would be perfectly holy.

So, then, there's really no such "thing" as grace; there is only Jesus. Sinclair Ferguson explains,

> There isn't a thing, a substance, or a "quasi-substance" called "grace." All there is is the person of the Lord Jesus—"Christ clothed in the gospel," as John Calvin

loved to put it. Grace is the grace of Jesus. If I can high-light the thought here: there is no "thing" that Jesus takes from Himself and then, as it were, hands over to me. There is only Jesus Himself. . . . It is not a thing that was crucified to give us a thing called grace. It was the person of the Lord Jesus that was crucified in order that He might give Himself to us through the ministry of the Holy Spirit.[8]

Salvation is all of grace and grace alone, by which we mean salvation is all of Christ and Christ alone!

It is from this wellspring of effervescent joy that we may cry out in the words of the grace-full hymn:

> Free from the law, O happy condition,
> Jesus hath bled, and there is remission;
> Cursed by the law and bruised by the fall,
> Grace hath redeemed us, once for all.
> Once for all, O sinner receive it,
> Once for all, O friend, now believe it;
> Cling to the cross, the burden will fall,
> Christ hath redeemed us once for all.[9]

This is the cry of one who has discovered that the plague every legalist fears, the scourge of the Roman Catholic Church, and the dread of her papacy is in fact the most wonderful and the most wondrous condition ever to "infect" anybody. When more of the reality of *sola gratia* settles into our soul, the more freedom we feel—not to sin, but to celebrate.

This leads us to the fourth and final *sola* remaining in the chain. How does *sola gratia* connect to *soli Deo gloria*?

GRACE ALONE PROCLAIMS
THE GLORY OF GOD ALONE

If we do not hold on to salvation by grace alone, we in effect disgrace grace and steal glory from God.

> Why then was the law given? It was added for the sake of transgressions until the Seed to whom the promise was made would come. The law was put into effect through angels by means of a mediator. Now a mediator is not just for one person alone, but God is one. (Gal. 3:19–20 CSB)

The Law was put in place via angels, through Moses. We see this affirmed in Acts 7:38 and 53, and in Hebrews 2:2. Deuteronomy 33:2 tells us it came to Sinai by "ten thousand holy ones" (CSB). That's a pretty impressive scene. "A mediator is not just for one person," Paul says. There were several links in the chain of command: from God via His ten thousand holy ones to Moses, then to the people. And let's not forget to factor in the priests and the ceremonial rites and regulations that went along with all that. In order to deliver—and then to administer—the Law, "teamwork," as they say, "makes the dream work."

"But," Galatians 3:20 says, "God is one."

Why is the gospel better than the Law? Why is Jesus more glorious than any other intermediary? Because it is God Himself doing the job Himself for the people Himself *all by Himself*. Consider the exhaustive and exhausting comprehensiveness and rigor that the Law entails. Multiply that by the glory that radiated on Moses' face, that was transmitted on a mountaintop via ten thousand flaming angels. Multiply that by precise measurements, a routine cycle of sacrifices, and an every-T-crossed attention to detail. Now consider that Christ Jesus is more glorious, more precise, more fulfilling, more encompassing than all that. And then! Consider that Jesus doesn't just hold up His end of the covenant of righteousness: He holds up our end too. An intermediary implies more than one. But God is one. He does His job, *and ours*. The Law is good (for what it's designed to do), but Jesus is much, much better.

And if salvation was by the law, we could do some boasting. But because salvation is all of grace—by grace alone—God does all the work and, therefore, God gets all the credit, all the glory.

Essentially, the gospel most glorifies God because it announces that God has saved us from Himself to Himself through Himself by Himself for Himself. Grace alone proclaims the glory of God alone.

3

FAITH ALONE
Jason G. Duesing

C. S. Lewis's *The Silver Chair* begins just like the three preceding Narnia books.[1] Following a suspenseful event, children in England find themselves transported to the magical land through an extraordinary doorway. Yet what makes the story of *The Silver Chair* unique is what happens when they arrive.

In this story, the cousin of the children in the earlier tales, Eustace Scrubb, and his friend, Jill Pole, are talking at school and Eustace tells her about this land to which he has traveled and together they start calling Aslan, the Lion lord of Narnia, to ask if they can return. As they are talking, they are chased by some other schoolmates and they run to a door and open it only to find they are in Narnia.

There they find they are in a forest at the edge of a cliff and, long story short, after a moment, Eustace falls off the cliff, and before Jill knows what happened, the lion Aslan appears and doesn't roar or speak, but rather breathes—and he, in effect, breathes wind strong enough to capture Eustace and send him further and safely into Narnia. Bewildered, Jill turns and encounters the Lion, who gives her a task and then explains that he will send her into Narnia via his breath, just as he sent Eustace.

Aslan commands, "Walk before me to the edge of the cliff." So the girl walks to the edge with nothing between her and the depths but a powerful Lion. "But long before she had got anywhere near the edge, the voice behind her said, 'Stand still.'" And Aslan reminded her of his instructions.

Lewis then explains that as the Lion's voice grew softer, "To [Jill's] astonishment she saw the cliff already more than a hundred yards behind her, and the Lion himself a speck of bright gold on the edge of it. She had been setting her teeth and clenching her fists for a terrible blast of lion's breath; but the breath had really been so gentle that she had not even noticed the moment at which she left the earth [and]. . . . floating on the breath of the lion was so extremely comfortable. She found she could lie on her back or on her face and twist any way she pleased, just as you can in water."

Jill Pole was passive, along for the ride on the vessel or bridge of the breath of a Lion. She was delivered by word-speaking-breath alone to Narnia. She would never think of boasting that she crossed that cavern of air on her own strength, yet she traveled in responsive obedience to the Lion's command. Further, she was sent to do good works, but her good tasks were the fruit of what she would do after she was transported by breath alone, not the cause.

Aside from acknowledging the journey across the divide, she did not conclude that she had nothing more to do once she arrived—far from it. She didn't set off following her own desires or sit and do nothing. Rather, it was clear she was transported for a purpose. Further, she could receive no praise for delivering herself to Narnia, all credit clearly had to go to the Lion.

Aslan's delivery of Jill to Narnia is a helpful picture of what the Bible articulates as saving faith and what the Protestant Reformers called *sola fide* or faith alone. What is more, for those of us living in the twenty-first century, how one understands the relationship of their faith in Christ and their obedience to Christ makes all the difference for living a life of joy and God-glorifying freedom. To gain a better grasp on what faith alone means, we will first consider what the Bible says in Romans 1:16–17. Next, to provide historical context and illustration, we will examine how faith alone played an instrumental role in the conversion of a Roman Catholic monk, Martin Luther. Finally, we will summarize how faith alone serves the believer well for all that God asks of us in the present day.

BIBLICAL FOUNDATION: ROMANS 1:16–17

"For I am not ashamed of the gospel, for it is the power of God for salvation to everyone who believes, to the Jew first and also to the Greek. For in it the righteousness of God is revealed from faith for faith, as it is written, 'The righteous shall live by faith'" (Rom. 1:16–17).

Even though these two verses played a powerful role in the life of Martin Luther and in the Protestant Reformation, they have held towering influence among the people of God since the Holy Spirit inspired Paul to write them.[2] Arguably, these two verses function as the core of Paul's letter to the Romans and, perhaps, even a central summary of the entire New Testament.

In verse 16, Paul first gives a negative expression. Here, he explains why he is "not" ashamed of the gospel.

Paul is not ashamed of the gospel, for the gospel is good news. While the gospel will always be offensive in a troubled world that regards it as foolishness, it is indeed good, as the word "gospel" means "good news." In this sense, the gospel transcends opinion and stands apart from evaluation. As philosopher Roger Scruton remarks, this is why medieval theologian Thomas Aquinas counted things from God that are true, beautiful, and good as "transcendentals," meaning that some gifts from God are more real than the world can comprehend and, thus, that their goodness does not change, but that we change to comprehend them.[3]

Paul is not ashamed of the gospel, for the gospel is from God's power. Even though many may mock the claims of Christ and His disciples, the gospel is a gift from God and not reliant upon the power of man. As Martyn Lloyd-Jones explains, "The gospel is not an encouragement to self-effort; it is the announcement of what God has done in order to save us."[4] Paul is not ashamed of that which declares the strength and kindness of God.

Paul is not ashamed of the gospel, for the gospel is effective to save. Of all the religions and non-religions of the world, the gospel of Jesus Christ is the only message that truly saves. That is, in their simplest form, all other ways of seeking to explain and understand the world are a call to look within and work out either peace with God or the obtaining of joy from one's own effort. While some may, more or less, allow a person to find less stress or more relational harmony, they cannot cleanse from sin or make a person right with the Creator of the universe. Only the gospel provides salvation from judgment.

Paul is not ashamed of the gospel, for the gospel saves everyone who believes. The declaration of the good news that God so loved the world that He gave His only Son, that whoever believes in Him should not perish (John 3:16) means that truly there is no hopeless person on the planet. God is able to save and will save everyone who believes.

Paul is not ashamed of the gospel, for the gospel is for all peoples. He makes the point that the gospel came not only to the Jews, but also to the non-Jews. When God told Abraham one night to look up and number the stars, for that is the number of his offspring (Gen. 15:5), God revealed that He had a plan to provide salvation for all the nations of the earth. Thus, Paul can declare that in Christ Jesus, Abraham's offspring, there is "neither Jew nor Greek" (Gal. 3:28) and give hope to everyone created in the image of God, regardless of where they were born or who are their parents.

In verse 17, by contrast, Paul gives a positive expression, explaining what is in the gospel for those who believe.

In the gospel, there is revelation. Reading the first two verses of Romans, we learn that God "promised beforehand through his prophets" the gospel (1:1–2). In his letter to the Galatians, Paul explains what we noted above, that the gospel was preached "beforehand to Abraham" (3:8) in Genesis 15. Likewise, here in Romans 1:17, Paul quotes another Old Testament text, Habakkuk 2:4 to support his teaching on the nature of the gospel. While the gospel was not revealed in full in the Old Testament, it was foreshadowed for those who lived at that time and for future believers. Paul reminds in 1 Corinthians that the Old Testament was written down for our instruction (10:11). The people of God in the Old Testament believed what was revealed to them and looked forward by faith in God's promises. We read what has been fully revealed in Jesus Christ and look backward by faith in God's promises. All of this is to remind us that the good news about Jesus Christ comes through a revealing from God, and this is another facet of the brilliant uniqueness of Christianity. The news of the way of salvation comes not through a discovery of golden tablets or making a pilgrimage—no, the gospel was revealed at the right time by God Himself to us.

In the gospel, God's righteousness is given. As we will see, the phrase "righteousness of God" was a stumbling block for Martin Luther and might be for many others as well. Some have thought Paul is merely declaring that God is righteous—that righteousness is His divine and perfect attribute—and thus distant and removed from sinful humanity. That is, Paul is declaring how God has revealed Himself as right and good and perfect, which He is, and that He demands such from His creation, but without any remedy for the contrasting wrong and evil humanity. However, upon a closer look, we see that the meaning here is that God's righteousness, perfect and unstained, is transferred, shared, and given to sinful humanity. How can a sinful man be made right before a perfect God? Paul is declaring here in verse 17 that in Christ, God gives His own righteousness and thus meets all His demands for perfection. As Paul says in 2 Corinthians 5:21, God made Jesus to be sin "so that in him we might become the righteousness of God." And in Philippians 3:9, he shares that human beings actually can receive God's perfect righteousness "through faith in Christ." Jesus Christ lived a perfect life, died to provide a perfect sacrifice, and thereby paid the perfect price to provide a transfer of the perfection God requires to sinful humanity.

In the gospel, faith alone is the vessel. How does this transfer happen? How does God's righteousness, the very thing we need most, become ours? Paul explains, by faith alone (*sola fide*). What then is faith? Faith in the New Testament is something that is given by God and is not present in every human being from birth. When it comes to thinking about faith, as the term is often used outside of a biblical understanding, many metaphors abound, but most are not helpful. I'd like to consider three examples.

First, Lloyd-Jones explains that comparing faith to flying on an airplane is not faith. One might say it takes a great deal of faith to enter a steel tube, piloted by a human being, traveling hundreds of miles in the air, but that is not faith—it is trusting in mathematical probability. That is, flying makes sense logically according to the laws of physics and math, and, therefore, one can rationalize why it is safe to fly.

Similarly, faith is not some lighter or easier path than the law. Oftentimes, Christians think that faith is the New Testament "Plan B" for the failed Old Testament "Plan A." God's people could not fulfill or keep the law, and, therefore, God provided a new plan around the law, "by faith." This is a common thought, but it is not consistent with the teaching of the entire Bible. In the Bible, we see that the law is good and is fulfilled perfectly in Christ. Believers in Christ meet the demands of the law through faith in him. By faith, they enter a relationship with God through the law, not around it, in Christ.

Third, faith is not what is required for salvation. Christians often mistakenly think what they need is simply more faith. This treats faith like a sizeable commodity and ultimately makes faith a work—and salvation comes not by works but *through* faith (Eph. 2:9). Faith is the opposite of legalism or trying to earn or work our way to God's righteousness. God's righteousness is given through faith alone, and faith itself is not what justifies us. Christ's righteousness is what makes us right and that comes *through* faith. Put another way, through faith alone we are made righteous, and that new righteousness produces fruit and good works and allows us then to live "by faith" after we are saved "through faith." Good works follow faith alone.

A more helpful metaphor is to think of faith as a bridge. Faith is the bridge over which we cross to salvation. It is the channel through which we sail, or the vessel on which we travel to salvation. In Romans 1:17, Paul's use of the phrase "from faith for faith" could be translated as "by faith to faith"—that is, God reveals His righteousness by the faith He gives to our faith. In other words, God's righteousness comes as a gift from God, and we are saved by Christ through this gift of faith alone.

In the gospel, there are now "the righteous." When Paul quotes Habakkuk 2:4 that the "righteous shall live by his faith," we should not miss the gloriousness of this statement. At the most basic and important level, he is declaring that there can, in fact, be humans that are "the righteous."[5] Human beings, you and I, can be justified, cleared, pardoned, cleansed, forgiven, rescued, and made right before God. Through faith in the life, death, and resurrection of Jesus—His atoning sacrifice and substitution on our behalf—we can have God's righteousness. But this comes only through faith alone, the gift of God.

HISTORICAL AND THEOLOGICAL CONTEXT

The year 2017 saw much focus on the 500th anniversary of the Protestant Reformation. From books, to conferences, to study tours, to public debate—there were endless opportunities to celebrate and learn more about what many, myself included, consider the greatest revival among God's people in history since the start of the church in Acts 2. And any discussion about the start of the Reformation cannot adequately take place without also discussing the leading Reformer, Martin Luther. While Luther was born in 1483, he started his "protest" against Roman Catholic theological and political corruption in 1517, hence the 500th anniversary. From that day until now, the figure of Luther has been lauded and vilified. In most theological libraries, there are more books on Luther than any other human other than Jesus— and Luther's books have been burned over the years, as his name is seen as synonymous with disgrace and division. Yet 500 years later, Luther cannot and should not be ignored.

Thus, to discuss the doctrine of faith alone, I want to draw attention to Luther's life and the Reformation, for the Reformation was not only world changing, but also, and especially, heart changing for Luther. For, at the heart of Luther's Reformation was how God first transformed his own heart—and the doctrines developed from there are really what made this movement so powerful.

To a Monastery. In 1505, Martin Luther was traveling alone and encountered a terrible thunderstorm. Read how Roland Bainton famously describes the scene:

> On a sultry day in July of the year 1505 a lonely traveler
> was trudging over a parched road on the outskirts of
> the Saxon village of Stotternheim. He was a young
> man, short but sturdy, and wore the dress of a university
> student. As he approached the village, the sky became
> overcast. Suddenly there was a shower, then a crashing

storm. A bolt of lightning rived the gloom and knocked the man to the ground. Struggling to rise, he cried in terror, "St. Anne help me! I will become a monk."

The man who thus called upon a saint was later to repudiate the cult of saints. He who vowed to become a monk was later to renounce monasticism. A loyal son of the Catholic Church, he was later to shatter the structure of medieval Catholicism. A devoted servant of the pope, he was later to identify the popes with Antichrist. For this young man was Martin Luther.[6]

The fourteenth and fifteenth centuries in Europe were a time of great anxiety over death due to regular plagues and the tremendous changes taking place economically and politically. Luther was like most young men living during this time except in two ways that heightened his anxiety: (1) he was given to mood changes and often suffered periods of depression; (2) he was more religiously inclined than the average youth around him. Therefore, what Luther feared in the thunderstorm was not death, but rather not being prepared for death.[7] That lightning strike had the effect of startling this Roman Catholic to determine that he needed to become a monk to make himself acceptable in the sight of God.

A Divine Shortcut to the Bible. Medieval people thought that monasticism was the avenue that could bring one closest to God and that monks would receive preferential treatment in heaven. Luther's sensitive conscience drove him to give himself completely to the monastic way of life. He thought that the strictest he could be as a monk would cause God to grant him favor. As a result, he came close to destroying his health with self-discipline. Luther stood in awe of the holiness and justice of God while deeply aware of his own sin. As he pursued asceticism to earn God's favor, he would ask how he could be certain he had done enough.[8]

At this point, Luther still believed that through confession and penance, sins could be forgiven. But he discovered that it was impossible for him to confess all his sins. This realization drove him to the point of murmuring against and then expressing hatred toward God for requiring a standard of holiness he could not obtain. After some time, Luther transferred to Wittenberg and met his new monk superior, Johann von Staupitz. Staupitz mentored Luther as a counselor, listening to all of Luther's fears and anxieties, and prompted him to consider further academic studies to allow him to teach at the University of Wittenberg. The teaching opportunity came with pastoral responsibilities and, thus, Staupitz's shepherding put Luther in a position of focusing on the doubts and needs of others in the hopes that Luther's doubts might subside.[9] The hidden providence in this wandering path of Luther's labors opened a shortcut that took him straight to the Bible. Staupitz's advice led Luther to the Scriptures, and as Luther would later say, "The Word did it all."[10]

Luther gave himself fully to the study of the Bible, and between 1513 and 1517, he had lectured on the Psalms, Romans, and Galatians, and particularly, the study of Romans made all the difference. Regarding Romans, Luther would later say, "[It is] the very purest Gospel, and is worthy not only that every Christian should know it word for word, by heart, but occupy himself with it every day, as the daily bread of the soul. It can never be read or pondered too much, and the more it is dealt with the more precious it becomes, and the better it tastes."[11] The fruit of Luther's study of Paul's precious letter appeared in the answer to the question that many have asked: "What must I do to be saved?" (Acts 16:30). The Reformation doctrine of "faith alone" is the answer to a question.

Luther's Discovery of Faith Alone. Luther's discovery of faith alone came as the result of his wrestling with the Holy Spirit over the God-breathed words of the apostle Paul in Romans 1:17. He came again to that verse, hating God and burdened by the weight of his inability to achieve God's standards. But after an epiphany, Luther underwent a dramatic transformation of his mind, heart, and understanding of that verse and of God Himself. Later, he would write,

> I had indeed been captivated with an extraordinary ardor for understanding Paul in the Epistle to the Romans. But until then it was not the cold blood about the heart, but a single word in Chapter 1[:17], "In it the righteousness of God is revealed," that had stood in my way. For I hated that word 'righteousness of God,' which, according to the use and custom of all the teachers, I had been taught to understand philosophically regarding the formal or active righteousness, as they

called it, with which God is righteous and punishes the unrighteous sinner.

Though I was a monk without reproach, I felt that I was a sinner before God with an extremely disturbed conscience. I could not believe that he was placated by my satisfaction. I did not love, yes, I hated the righteous God who punishes sinner, and secretly, if not blasphemously, certainly murmuring greatly, I was angry with God. . . .

At last, by the mercy of God, meditating day and night, I gave heed to the context of the words, namely, "In it the righteousness of God is revealed, as it is written, 'He who through faith is righteous shall live.'" There I began to understand that the righteousness of God is that by which the righteous lives by a gift of God, namely by faith. And this is the meaning: the righteousness of God is revealed by the gospel, namely the passive righteousness with which merciful God justifies us by faith, as it is written, "He who through faith is righteous shall live." Here I felt that I was altogether born again and had entered paradise itself through open gates. There a totally other face of the entire Scripture showed itself to me. Thereupon I ran through the Scriptures from memory. . . .

And I extolled by sweetest word with a love as great as the hatred with which I had before hated the word "righteousness of God." Thus that place in Paul was for me truly the gate to paradise.[12]

Luther likened his conversion to discovering the gate to paradise, which is a remarkable image.

My entire life, I have loved the game of baseball. Since age four, the first time I recall understanding what the World Series is, I have been particularly fond of the New York Yankees. Yet it was not until the eighth grade that I first saw Yankee Stadium in person. I can remember even now, clearly, walking through the stands on the first base side, through a tunnel, and coming out and looking down on the field. Don Mattingly was taking ground balls at first base, and over to the left was home plate—and when I saw that vacant part of the stadium, it hit me. There, on that very spot, once stood every great Yankee from Ruth to DiMaggio to Gehrig to Mantle to Berra. I had been a fan for many years, had seen games on television, but there was nothing like seeing for myself the actual place where the Yankees played. Seeing it in person was surreal, like someone had opened a gate through that first base tunnel to paradise—or at least an enclosed garden of sorts.

This boyhood experience times a million is what Luther experienced when he found his gate to paradise and was born again. From these early years, Luther developed and expounded the idea of salvation by grace alone through faith alone, and the world has never been the same.

FIVE SUMMARY STATEMENTS

Building upon this biblical and historical foundation, we can draw five summary statements from the eternal truths of the doctrine of faith alone for the present day.

1. Faith Alone is contrary to works-based legalism on the one hand and easy believism (or antinomianism) on the other. The Bible teaches that faith is not a work and that salvation does not come through human work. When the legalist demands "more faith" or any kind of good works as criteria by which God will accept fallen humanity, the doctrine of faith alone says, "No," and points to the work of Christ. Or when the minimalist assures that regardless of how one lives, if they've said the right things, they surely are safe from God's judgement, the doctrine of faith alone says, "No," and points to the biblical evidence that salvation by grace alone though faith alone always results in good works and the desire to obey God. Faith alone stands as a steady guide for freedom and joyful living for the believer walking with God.

2. Faith Alone is not a novel idea. The Old Testament articulates salvation through faith alone even as it looks through a glass dimly toward the revealing of the gospel in Jesus Christ.

The New Testament articulates salvation through faith alone on its own based on the fully revealed work of Christ (see Col. 1:26). The development of doctrine among Christian churches following the New Testament saw the early church fathers express aspects of faith alone, but not with the clarity of the Reformers. The Reformers, especially Luther and Calvin, are unified on the doctrine of faith alone, and the later evangelical tradition is built upon this same understanding of faith alone. That said, the New Testament articulation of faith alone doesn't need the clarification of Luther, Calvin, or evangelicals for clarity or to make certain texts in the Bible clearer.[13]

3. Faith Alone is still a Protestant distinctive. While some evangelicals and Roman Catholics have had helpful dialogues about the doctrine of faith alone,[14] and while some Lutherans and Catholics have had some more confusing conversations,[15] the Council of Trent, the *Catechism of the Catholic Church*, and other official teachings reveal that clear differences in understanding exist between Roman Catholics and Protestants. While there are differences still on a variety of terms, the divide primarily centers on the word "alone."[16] Roman Catholics agree that Scripture is authoritative and inspired, but in terms of biblical authority outweighing tradition, they do not believe in Scripture alone. Roman Catholics agree that for salvation, sinners need Christ by grace through faith. But they also believe that sinful humans can cooperate with grace in order to earn salvation. For them, faith is closely connected with works for justification. They also believe that one adds his or her own sacramental work, as well as those of Mary and the saints, to the sacrificial work of Christ. They do not believe in Christ alone, grace alone, and faith alone. Roman Catholics agree that glory should go to God for what He has done in salvation, but they cannot believe in glory to God alone, for salvation comes, in part, to what man does.[17] In short, the Reformation is not over. For Protestants, marked by *sola*, "One little word still compels them."[18]

4. Faith Alone should produce humility. I tell my students that one of the most important areas in which to grow is in humility. The doctrine of faith alone helps us cultivate humility, because it reminds us that salvation from God is a gift "so that no one may boast" (Eph. 2:9). As the great curator of the Inklings collection at Wheaton College, Clyde Kilby resolved, "I shall not demean my own uniqueness by envy of others. I shall stop boring into myself to discover what psychological or social categories I might belong to. Mostly I shall simply forget about myself and do my work."[19] Salvation by faith alone frees the Christian to no longer fixate on the self and instead to focus on Christ and others.[20]

5. Faith Alone should fuel evangelism and the Great Commission. Once we realize that if our lives have been transformed by the gift of salvation by faith alone in Christ alone so that we are made righteous before God, we have received the very thing every other human being on the planet needs. While sharing the good news is just that simple, we often overcomplicate evangelism. Every human being that God brings into our lives, He brings for a purpose—and all of those human beings need the righteousness of God to be saved. If your life has been changed, tell them about it. As you go to work, as you travel around the world, tell them the gospel and make disciples of them. His blood can make the foulest clean, by faith alone, His blood availed for me.

A WONDERFUL MYSTERY

To be sure, there is still a mystery in how God works and gives us faith and saves us. And, in time, that final mystery will all be made clear. Still, let us recall C. S. Lewis's *The Silver Chair*. We started by recounting Jill's first encounter with Aslan before he sent her on her way to Narnia on nothing but his own breath. In that moment, Aslan explains he was the one who had called them back to Narnia. Hearing this, Jill actually protests and explains that no one called them, and that they asked to go there. Aslan kindly replies, "You would not have called to me unless I had been calling to you." After he calls them, he gives them an assignment to do good works, and commissions them to go to Narnia via the vessel of his own breathed out words.

God calls us, gives us faith—a beautiful vessel, a bridge—through which He gives us His righteousness in Christ. Saved by faith alone, we are made new and sent forth to do good works for His glory.

4

CHRIST ALONE
Matthew Barrett

Toward the end of the nineteenth century, the *London Times* published a story about the hymn writer Augustus Toplady (1740–1778). Reportedly, Toplady was traveling when suddenly he was "overtaken by a heavy thunderstorm in Burrington Coombe [England], . . . a rocky glen . . . and there, taking shelter between two massive pillars of our native limestone, he penned the hymn, 'Rock of Ages, Cleft for Me.'"[1]

> Rock of Ages, cleft for me,
> let me hide myself in thee;
> let the water and the blood,
> from thy wounded side which flowed,

be of sin the double cure;
save from wrath and make me pure.

Not the labors of my hands
can fulfill thy law's commands;
could my zeal no respite know,
could my tears forever flow,
all for sin could not atone;
thou must save, and thou alone.

Nothing in my hand I bring,
simply to the cross I cling;
naked, come to thee for dress;
helpless, look to thee for grace;
foul, I to the fountain fly;
wash me, Savior, or I die.

While I draw this fleeting breath,
when mine eyes shall close in death,
when I soar to worlds unknown,
see thee on thy judgment throne,
Rock of Ages, cleft for me,
let me hide myself in thee.

Most people do not believe the story from the *London Times* is credible. Regardless, Toplady's hymn still vividly captures the central belief of the Reformation. What is that belief? It is summarized in the Reformation *sola* "Christ alone" (*solus Christus*). Although we have nothing but sin in our hands, and although we stand before the throne of God naked, we are washed by the blood of our Savior and clothed in His robe of righteousness. Even in the face of death itself, the believer trusting in Christ alone can rest assured that he is safe in the arms of Christ, hid in the Rock of Ages.

The thunderstorm story surrounding Toplady may be mythological, but over 200 years prior to Toplady there was a young German by the name of Martin Luther who really was caught in a thunderstorm. Unlike Toplady, young Martin had yet to discover "Christ alone," and so he was filled with overwhelming angst in the face of death. He believed every lightning bolt was an expression of God's wrath and any minute the devil would have his soul. Petrified, Martin cried out, vowing to become a monk, all in an effort to somehow save his soul.[2]

In that moment of desperation, one would never guess that God would use this trembling man to change the world and recover the gospel to the church. But after years of trying to merit favor with God—nearly going mad in the process—Luther's eyes were opened to one revolutionary fact: the righteousness he sought was not to be found within; it was none other than the righteousness of Christ, given as a gift to all who believe. Over time, the righteousness of God that Luther so feared and hated became his greatest comfort. Only faith in Christ alone could free Luther's burdened conscience. Luther was like Christian in John Bunyan's *Pilgrim's Progress*; finally, the burden on his back had been lifted. Liberated, Luther would risk his neck to tell others this good news. The Babylonian captivity of the church was over.[3]

THE BABYLONIAN CAPTIVITY
OF THE ROMAN CHURCH

Today, we look back at sixteenth-century giants like Martin Luther and John Calvin, and consider them "Reformers." But we should not forget that there was a time when a young Martin and John were *not yet* Reformers. Early on, they were raised to assume Rome's view of salvation was correct. Remember, Martin came of age in the early fifteenth century, which means he was a late medieval man living in a late medieval world, breathing the air of a late medieval view of salvation. So what type of theology did a young Martin Luther and John Calvin imbibe?[4]

It was believed that one must begin with man's nature and move upward to God's grace. After the fall in Genesis 3, sin distorted man's nature, but was not so debilitating that man was unable to cooperate with grace. In theology, this cooperation is called "synergism." Mankind after Adam may be injured by sin's effects, losing the original righteousness Adam possessed; nevertheless, man is not so crippled that he cannot do his best to perform works of merit and cooperate with or resist grace.

But what kind of grace is it that God gives? In this view, it is a grace that is infused into man's nature, so that more and more man's nature is inherently changed, lifted up until it finally reaches God, being deified and divinized. Becoming right with God, then, is not strictly a matter of being declared right with God, instantly having a new status in Christ. Rather, it is a process by which one is made intrinsically righteous through the infusion of grace into one's nature. Such an infusion was essential if man is to merit the remission of his sins and eternal life.

Where does one receive such grace? The Church, specifically Rome (and only Rome). Christ has ascended into heaven, so the Church is Christ on earth, ensuring that our natures are being made righteous until they reach God. The Church is the God-appointed, infallible mediator of infused grace. Outside the Roman Church there is no salvation; outside her walls no infused grace can be found. As much as Christ is man's exclusive Savior, the Church is needed as mediator of the grace that Christ gives. Salvation cannot be based upon the work of Christ *alone* (*solus Christus*); rather, Christ is in the church (*Christus in ecclesia*), and the church is in Christ (*ecclesia in Christo*).[5] Simple trust in Christ is not enough.

How, then, does one receive grace from the Church? Answer: the sacraments.[6] The word *sacrament* comes from the Latin *sacramentum*. It refers to the consecration of something, and in Rome's understanding the sacraments act as channels through which grace flows down to those in the pew. Three sacraments are especially important: baptism, the Eucharist, and penance. Let's consider each.

For Rome, baptism is an event that carries power and cannot be repeated. Washing away original sin, baptism is capable of remitting both the guilt (*culpa*) and punishment (*poena*) inherited from Adam at the fall. So powerful are the waters of baptism that some believed if one died immediately after baptism one would go straight to heaven, rather than having to go to purgatory first. Baptism initially transitioned someone from a state of sin to a state of grace. Unfortunately, everyone sins after baptism, so one must do penance to cover post-baptismal sins against God. We will return to penance later.

Another channel of grace is the Eucharist. The focal point of the Mass liturgy was the altar, which stood at the head of the church, a table to the bread and wine. Upon saying the liturgy of the Mass, the substance of the bread and wine are transformed into the blood and flesh of Christ, even though the appearance of the bread and wine (what medieval theology called the "accidents") continued to look the same. A transubstantiation occurs in that holy moment. By Luther's day, the Church withheld the wine from the people for a variety of reasons, one of them being the fear of spilling the wine, defiling the blood of the Lord.[7]

Sacraments, including the Eucharist, not only distribute grace but do so automatically, regardless of whether the priest is holy or whether the recipient has faith. There is a Latin phrase that communicates this belief: *ex opere operato*, which means "by the work performed." Again, like baptism, there is a power here, so that unless the recipient intentionally puts up a barrier between himself and the Eucharist, the elements confer grace simply by being given. The performance of Mass was that powerful.[8] While the Reformers said faith must be present, the Council of Trent, which was Rome's official response to the Reformers, denied that the "sacraments have been instituted for the nourishment of faith alone."

For Rome, the sacraments "contain the grace that they signify," and they actually "confer that grace upon those who do not place obstacles in its path." Trent issued this condemnation of the Reformers: "If anyone says that the sacraments . . . do not confer grace *ex opere operato*, but that faith alone in the divine promise is sufficient to obtain grace, let them be condemned."[9] Now here is the meat of the nut, the dividing line between Rome and the Reformers. For the Reformers, all that is required is faith alone, which itself is a gift from the Spirit who enables the believer to trust in the promises of God in the gospel of His Son, promises visibly confirmed, signified, and sealed in the Eucharist.[10] But for Rome, faith alone in the saving work of Christ alone is not enough. The Eucharist itself must confer grace, and it does so only when the priest performs the Mass. In short, the priest's performance is no mere celebration but is itself a good work.[11]

Just as significant was the sacrament of penance, which was deeply ingrained in the ordinary life of any late medieval man or woman. As mentioned earlier, sins after baptism explained why it was so crucial to receive infused grace from the church through channels like the Eucharist. Baptism, remember, could not be repeated. So, penance became key, because unlike baptism, penance is repeatable. But penance is not as powerful as baptism. While it removes guilt, it can only lessen punishment from eternal punishment to a temporary punishment.[12] This temporal punishment must be satisfied through the process of penance.

What does this process entail? Penance involves several steps:

1. *Contrition*: The sinner has authentic sorrow or remorse for sin; one is penitent.

2. *Confession (and absolution)*: The sinner confesses his/ her sins to a priest; the priest grants absolution for one's guilt.

3. *Satisfaction*: The priest assigns work(s) of satisfaction (fasting, giving alms to the poor, prayers, pilgrimages, masses, indulgences, etc.) to pay off one's temporal punishment.

But what should happen if one dies before he can complete satisfaction for the temporal punishment of his sins? That question is a strange one because everyone, except for Mary and the holiest of saints, died in such a state. Suffering is almost always necessary in a place of purgation (Purgatory) to suffer until satisfaction is met and one has been purged and made righteous to enter heaven's gates.

"THE COIN IN THE COFFER RINGS, THE SOUL FROM PURGATORY SPRINGS"

Yet by Luther's day, there was a shortcut that came to be abused. The pope had issued an indulgence slip that one could purchase to lessen years in purgatory. This was genius because an indulgence could release you from those many works of satisfaction you were obligated to fulfill.

Here's how it worked: Rome recognized that Mary and the saints did so many good works that they had an overabundance amount of merit. Pooled together, these good works made up the treasury of merit (sometimes called the treasury of the Church), a type of heavenly treasure chest. The pope of Luther's day determined that he had the right and the ability to transfer and apply merit from that treasury to anyone who bought an indulgence slip, either on their own behalf or on behalf of a dead loved one.

Technically, an indulgence is the full or partial remission of temporal punishment for sins. In Luther's day, the pope had issued a *plenary* indulgence: for the right price, *all* of one's temporal punishment could be removed! A man by the name of Johann Tetzel travelled from town to town abusing the indulgence system by laying the guilt trip on thick: "Listen to the voices of your dear dead relatives and friends, beseeching you and saying, 'Pity us, pity us. We are in dire torment from which you can redeem us for a pittance. . . . Will you let us lie here in flames? Will you delay our promised glory?'" Next Tetzel sang his catchy little jingle: "As soon as the coin in the coffer rings, the soul from purgatory springs."[13]

When Martin Luther discovered that many under his care were running off to buy indulgences and coming back believing they had just purchased heaven for their soul, he was outraged. "Evidently the poor souls believe that when they have bought indulgence letters they are then assured of their salvation. . . . O great God! The souls committed to your care, excellent Father, are thus directed to death. For all these souls you have the heaviest and a constantly increasing responsibility. Therefore I can no longer be silent on this subject."[14] In response, Luther drafted ninety-five theses protesting the abuse of indulgences. Although he intended these theses merely for academic debate, they were translated in the common language of German and spread across the country, even across Europe. The Reformation had begun, and it would unleash a theological firestorm no one ever anticipated.

REDISCOVERING "CHRIST ALONE"

As complicated as Rome's view of salvation may be, her debate with the Reformer's came down to one word: "alone." Sure, Rome believed that salvation was based upon the work of Christ, but she would not say that salvation was based upon the work of Christ *alone*. Christ alone, or *solus Christus* in Latin, may seem like a very small difference—one word!—but for the Reformer's, it was all the difference in the world. Upon this one word (*alone*) the whole gospel depended.

There were several ways in which the Reformers rediscovered "Christ alone." First, with the New Testament freshly translated from the Greek (rather than from the Latin), the Reformers stared at the text long enough to realize that when Paul referred to justification, he did not have in mind a process by which one is made inherently righteous by an internal, moral renewal. Justification, rather, is a legal matter. It is God's gracious and judicial declaration that we sinners are no longer guilty but righteous.

Second, this new legal status is not based upon anything in us or anything that we do but is entirely based upon what Christ has done for us. He has not only paid the penalty for our sins in full on the cross, but also lived a life of perfect obedience. Upon faith alone in Christ alone, not only is our sin forgiven in full, but Christ's flawless righteous status is imputed or reckoned to our account. Rome's belief that man needs an infusion of grace is a teaching without biblical foundation. What every guilty sinner needs is not an infusion but an imputation.

Third, when the Reformers rediscovered this biblical doctrine of justification, everything Rome taught was thrown into question. Sinners do not need to perform works of satisfaction to pay the temporal penalty for their sin; Christ paid that penalty in full on the cross. Sinners do not need to save up their monies to purchase an indulgence to receive the merits of the saints; Christ has obeyed the law on the sinner's behalf and given His perfect righteousness to sinners free of charge. One need not run to the priest for absolution; Christ is our high priest so that "if anyone does sin," he has "an advocate with the Father, Jesus Christ the righteous" (1 John 2:1).[15] And one need not run to the Mass presuming, said Calvin, "to sacrifice Christ anew!"; Christ's sacrifice is "never to be repeated," for it paid for our sin in full.[16]

And so, the Reformers boldly concluded, with the threat of execution hanging over their heads, that the ungodly are justified by grace alone (*sola gratia*), through faith alone (*sola fide*), on the basis of Christ alone (*solus Christus*).

WHY GOD BECAME MAN

Is "Christ alone" a *sola* that we find in the Scriptures? Yes, but to see it, we must, in contrast to Rome, start with a very different picture of man's nature.

There are few doctrines so fundamental to the storyline of Scripture as man's pervasive depravity. It frames the entire storyline of the Bible from Adam to Christ, it is central to the good news of a Savior announced at the opening of the Gospel narratives, and yet it is predictably evasive in the hands of the modern man. The reason is ironic: We don't think we are really as bad as Scripture says we are. We've convinced ourselves that we have made some "mistakes" here and there but that we surely are not as bad as others we see around us.

In the book of Romans, the apostle Paul addresses this deception, a lie we live and have persuaded ourselves is true. The reason such logic fails is because we are judging ourselves by the wrong standard. We look out on the world, find someone who has done something worse than us, and feel confident, reassuring ourselves we're not that bad in the end. But that is not how God looks at us. He does not compare us to others, but instead exposes the darkness of our hearts in the full brightness and blinding purity of His holiness. When we are examined according to the perfection of His moral character, what does He find?

"None is righteous, no, not one;
  no one understands;
  no one seeks for God.
All have turned aside; together they have become worthless;
  no one does good,
  not even one."
"Their throat is an open grave;
  they use their tongues to deceive."
"The venom of asps is under their lips."
  "Their mouth is full of curses and bitterness."
"Their feet are swift to shed blood;
  in their paths are ruin and misery,
and the way of peace they have not known."
  "There is no fear of God before their eyes."
(Rom. 3:10–18)

Paul's condemnation could not be more *universal*—it applies to everyone without exception. And by implication, Paul's verdict could not be more *pervasive*—there is no part of our humanity that escapes. The lips, throat, mouth, feet, and eyes—man's whole being—are instruments of depravity. So extensive is the corruption of man's nature.

And yet, as we've seen already with Rome, many today still try to find an antidote to the sin problem by looking within. "Yes, we need Christ. Yes, we need grace. And yes, we need faith. But surely there is still something within us that is worthy, or at least something within us that can still do something, even if it be slight, to earn favor in God's sight." So the argument goes.

What was so shocking about the Reformers was that they concluded, without qualification, that there is absolutely nothing within ourselves, even if assisted by grace, that can somehow merit God's favor or cooperate with God's grace. The antidote has nothing to do with us but must be external to us, alien to ourselves. No part of us, who are pervasively corrupt, escapes the clutches of sin's grip. Our mind, our affections, even our will—all fall under the corrupting impact of Adam's sin. The title of Luther's response to Erasmus says it all: *The Bondage of the Will.* Even that human faculty we consider the most autonomous—the will—is enslaved to sin, the world, and the devil. But Luther was saying nothing novel; he was simply echoing the apostle Paul before him: "You were dead in the trespasses and sins in which you once walked, following the course of this world, following the prince of the power of the air" (Eph. 2:1–2).

It is telling that Paul spends nearly the first three chapters of his letter to the Romans describing man's guilt and condemnation before the Creator, before he even begins to introduce the mercy and grace of God as Savior. It's only when we come to terms with our own utter unworthiness, inability, and depravity that we can even begin to understand why it was so necessary for God to become man. Having heard a resounding, heavenly declaration of one's guilty status before the divine judge (Rom. 1:18–3:20), Paul comes running into the celestial courtroom with the greatest of news: "All have sinned and fall short of the glory of God," but we guilty and condemned sinners "are justified by his grace as a gift, through the redemption that is in Christ Jesus, whom God put forward as a propitiation by his blood, to be received by faith" (3:23–25). Earlier, we noted that salvation could not come from *within*, but that the antidote had to be external, alien to ourselves. Here, we see Paul make the same point. Justification—God's legal declaration that we are not guilty but righteous in His sight—does not come from within; nor can we merit it. Rather, says Paul, we are justified "by his grace as a gift" (3:24).

"But wait a minute, Paul. How can this be? After all, we are guilty sinners, and God is holy. Surely, He cannot declare us just in His sight. To do so would compromise His own righteous character. How can the judge of all the earth not do what is right?" Did you notice that Paul says we are justified by God's "grace as a gift *through the redemption that is in Christ Jesus*"? The gift is only possible because the Son of God became man in order to redeem us. He did this, says Paul, by acting as our substitute. Taking our place, Christ took upon Himself the wrath of God that we deserved. The penalty for our guilt was placed upon Christ, and He bore it in full. Paul has a special word to describe Christ as our wrath-bearing substitute; it's the word "propitiation." We are justified by God's grace, which is a gift, only because "God put forward [Christ] as a propitiation by his blood" (3:25). "By faith," says Paul, we become the recipients of this blood-bought gift.

Apart from the cross, God would not be just to justify the ungodly. Our instinct—that God would compromise His righteousness to simply waive the penalty of the guilty—is right. However, it's not a problem for God since the Father put forward His own Son as an atoning sacrifice. He put forward Christ as our propitiation "to show God's righteousness, because in his divine forbearance he had passed over former since." Nevertheless, by putting Christ forward to bear the penalty for our sins, God is both "just and the justifier of the one who has faith in Jesus" (3:26). At the cross, justice and mercy meet and kiss one another.

THE GREAT EXCHANGE

In the Reformation tradition, we have a phrase that captures these great truths that we see in Romans 3: *the great exchange.* The great exchange is all about *who* represents you as you stand before God on judgment day.

As Paul explains in Romans 5, Adam was our first representative. Sadly, as our representative, when he sinned he plunged all humanity into condemnation with him. The guilt and corrupt nature of Adam have been imputed or reckoned to us, his posterity. This is the doctrine of original sin. As a result, our nature is now inclined toward sin rather than toward righteousness. Naturally, the first chance we get, we act upon our sinful inclinations and only increase our guilt before a holy God. We not only break God's law but fail to keep it perfectly as His perfect righteousness requires. Our predicament could not be worse.

But the beauty of the gospel is found in a Savior who succeeds where Adam failed. Like our first father, Adam, Christ also acts as our representative. But as the second or last Adam, he does not fall prey to the temptations of the evil one. His mission is twofold. On the one hand, he was born to die. Countless times in the Gospels, Jesus reveals His intention to lay down His life (for example, see Mark 10:45). Why? Because He must suffer the penalty for our law-breaking (transgression) if we are to be forgiven. Until He drinks the cup of divine wrath in full (see Mark 14:36), He cannot declare "It is finished" (John 19:30).

Yet there is a flip side to this gospel coin, this great exchange, and one many today fail to remember. It's not enough to merely have our sins forgiven, as essential as that may be. If only the penalty is paid, then we stand before God naked still. Yes, our guilty robe has been removed, but no positive righteousness speaks for us in the sight of a righteous God. Needed still, then, is the obedience of our Lord. Perhaps you've wondered before about the relevance of the life of Christ. You understand the cross, but why was an entire life necessary? It was necessary that Christ lived a perfect life of obedience where Adam had failed so that Christ's perfect record of obedience might be credited to our account. Remember, we've not only broken the law but failed to uphold the whole law perfectly. But not Christ. At no point in His ministry did He falter. At no juncture did His obedience to His Father wane. He went to the cross as the spotless Lamb of God. As a result, those who place their faith in Him alone are not only forgiven but declared righteous.

The righteousness that justifies, however, is not our own. How can it be? Rather, it is an alien righteousness. Or as Luther said, it is *extra nos*, apart from us. It is a righteousness given to us by Christ as a gift, and it is a righteousness that is Christ's own. That explains why Paul can say, "For our sake he [God] made him [Christ] to be sin who knew no sin, so that in him we might become the righteousness of God" (2 Cor. 5:21). Elsewhere, Paul will boast that he does not have "a righteousness of my own that comes from the law, but that which comes through faith in Christ" (Phil. 3:9). Such a righteousness means we no longer stand naked before the heavenly throne but are clothed in the robe of Christ's righteousness. When the Father looks at us, He sees the perfection of His Son and announces to all the world that we are no longer guilty but justified in His Son.

THE SACRIFICE TO END ALL SACRIFICES

So far, we've seen why it was so necessary for the Son of God to become incarnate, but a question lingers still: Is the work of Christ enough? Is it really sufficient? Or, as we saw with Rome, must something else—something within us or from the Church—accompany Christ's saving work, be added to it, and even finish it?

The author of Hebrews gives us a clear answer. In Hebrews 9, the author takes us back to the Old Testament and reminds us what life was like under the Law of Moses. Once a year, on the Day of Atonement, the high priest had the opportunity to enter the Most Holy Place to intercede for God's people (9:7–8). But he couldn't just waltz into the presence of the Holy. He needed not only the blood from sacrifices offered on behalf of the sins of the people, but blood to cover his own sins as well. Not even the high priest—who was probably the holiest person in Israel—could enter God's presence without the blood of atonement. Why was this bloody ritual so necessary? "Without the shedding of blood there is no forgiveness of sins" (9:22). Apart from a blood sacrifice, the wrath of the Holy One remains upon those who are rebels, idolaters, and transgressors of His holy law.

Actually, the problem is worse than you think. Hebrews tells us not only that blood sacrifices were necessary, but also that they did not last. They had to be made over and over again. Each year, the high priest had to enter the presence of God with more blood. Although these sacrifices allowed Israel to continue as God's covenant people, they were not sufficient. The "same sacrifices that are continually offered every year," says Hebrews, cannot "make perfect those who draw near"; if they could "would they not have ceased to be offered?" (10:1–2). "But in these sacrifices there is a reminder of sins every year. For it is impossible for the blood of bulls and goats to take away sins" (10:3–4).

What, then, will end this bloody cycle? The better question is *who* will bring this cycle to an end? None other than Jesus, the Christ. No one expected this. The Son of God Himself became incarnate, true God yet true man, to act as our great High Priest and enter into the Most Holy Place. But here is what is so astounding: He did so by means of *His own blood*. He needed no goat or bull. No, He offered up His own life as a sacrifice for sins. And He was qualified to do so because, unlike the priests before him, He was a priest who had not sinned, who needed no sacrifice for His own transgressions.

What made His sacrifice so unique was that it was not repeatable, unlike the countless sacrifices before Him. As the God-man, His blood was sufficient to pay for our sins once and for all. Only the eternal Son of God could pay for sins against an eternally holy God, sins deserving an eternal punishment in hell. If Christ's humanity enabled Him to represent fallen humanity, His divinity made Him alone capable of redeeming those deserving endless suffering. As we read in Hebrews, "When Christ appeared as a high priest . . . he entered once for all into the holy places, not by means of the blood of goats and calves but by means of *his own blood*, thus securing an *eternal* redemption"

(9:11–12; emphasis added). The author of Hebrews then concludes, "Therefore he is the mediator of a new covenant, so that those who are called may receive the promised eternal inheritance." (9:15). Christ did not need to "offer himself repeatedly, as the high priest enters the holy places every year with blood not his own, for then he would have had to suffer *repeatedly* since the foundation of the world." Rather, "he has appeared *once for all* at the end of the ages to put away sin by the sacrifice of himself" (9:25–26; emphasis added).

What the author of Hebrews is trying to convey is most profound: The believer has every assurance that the sacrifice of Christ is enough. No sin, no transgression, escapes the blood of Jesus. No idolatry, no matter how hideous, is a match for the power found in the blood of the Lamb. We have been redeemed by the blood of Christ *alone*, and His blood is enough, sufficient to pay for all our sins.

YOUR ONLY COMFORT
IN LIFE AND IN DEATH

Does "Christ alone" have any implications for the Christian life?

In my first year of teaching, I was assigned a theology class. At the end of one lecture, a middle-aged woman approached me, troubled and perplexed. She had grown up all her life in the Roman Catholic Church and, like young Martin Luther, never could find assurance. She never knew whether her works were good enough or whether her prayers were contrite enough. She did not know a gracious God. Yet she had evangelical cowork-ers who were full of assurance and joy, and this lady had no idea how that could be possible. With a smile on my face, I looked at her and said, "I have some great news to share with your anxious soul. Jesus has paid it all."

Of course, lack of assurance can be a serious struggle even for those who have believed in the gospel. As any pastor will tell you, many sheep who truly believe in Jesus struggle to retain that great comfort of full assurance. Some of the greatest Christians in the history of the church—hymn writers like William Cooper—struggled to retain assurance. What is the medicine that soul without assurance needs? Christ alone.

Satan loves to creep up and whisper into your ear: "You are a sinner. God will never accept you. We all know how hideous your sin is and just how guilty you are before God." Martin Luther himself says Satan approached him countless times, saying just that. The trouble is, Satan is right. We are unworthy, guilty, and condemned. Looking to ourselves will only deepen the dark hour of our soul. What Martin Luther discovered, however, is that Satan fled the minute he mentioned his Savior, Jesus Christ. Why? Because in Christ Jesus, every believer stands justified. Satan's accusations may be true, but when clothed in the perfect righteousness of Christ, they no longer have any power.

The Reformer John Calvin was a pastor in Geneva and in his lifetime he shepherded many with guilt-enslaved con-sciences. What was Calvin's medicine for these sick souls? Christ alone. "If we seek redemption, it lies in his [Christ's] passion;

if acquittal, in his condemnation; if remission of the curse, in his cross [Gal. 3:13]; if satisfaction, in his sacrifice; if purification, in his blood."[17] Distrust, Calvin concludes, "cannot creep in where men have once for all truly known the abundance of his [Christ's] blessings."[18] Calvin's point is captured by The Heidelberg Catechism (1563) when it asks, "What is your only comfort in life and in death?" Answer: "That I, with body and soul . . . am not my own, but belong to my faithful Savior Jesus Christ, who with His precious blood has fully satisfied for all my sins."[19] If you are crushed under the weight of sin with Satan's accusations pressing in, there is one word in that answer that will send sin and Satan running. It is the word "fully." The precious blood of Christ has "fully" satisfied all your sins. What greater assurance could there be? Faith alone in Christ alone, said Luther, "means peace of conscience."[20]

"Therefore, brothers, since we have confidence to enter the holy places by the blood of Jesus, by the new and living way that he opened for us . . . let us draw near with a true heart in full assurance of faith" (Heb. 10:19–22).

5

GLORY TO GOD ALONE
Owen Strachan

Eric Liddell ran with his head back, his mouth open, and a serene look on his face. He was just about the fastest man in the world, and one of the most famous. After gaining Olympic glory as a gold medalist, he had everything the natural human heart could want: the chance to become quite wealthy, positions at schools like Oxford, fame and influence that few would ever attain. But the runner immortalized in the movie *Chariots of Fire* passed all this by and gave all this up. He had other things on his mind. Specifically, he had God's glory in view.[1]

Liddell knew that ministering in God's kingdom was of inestimable value, both to God and man. He had a big heart for the work of missions and the making of disciples among people who had never heard of Christ. So, with the British Empire celebrating his victories and watching for his next move, Liddell took the most culturally counterintuitive step possible: he moved to China to be a poor missionary in a dusty, far-flung place. He taught school, engaged his neighbors, and showed kindness to many around him. Why did he do it? The answer might seem complicated, but in truth, it is simple: he did it for the glory. But not his glory.

The glory of God.

HOW THE REFORMATION RECOVERED A DOCTRINE OF DIVINE GLORY

If Liddell's station in life was unusual, his motive was not. The story of Eric Liddell speaks powerfully to a life set aside for God, dedicated to making God known and amplifying God's renown. Such a life fits with the great *sola* of the Reformation: *soli Deo gloria*, meaning we live "for God's glory alone." This, one of the five *solas* of the Reformation, sums up why we exist, and indeed, why all things exist: for God.[2]

Yet here we must boldly declare a quirk of history. The phrase *soli Deo gloria* was never uttered by the Reformers, though they certainly embraced the concept. Now well-known as the banner over the entire Reformational enterprise, the *sola* that points to the ultimate aim of true Christianity was never inscribed in a Luther text, commented on in a Calvin exegetical sermon, or mused over by Balthasar Hubmaier. In truth, none of these great Protestant leaders ever used this now-famous formulation.[3]

Instead, it was two musicians who introduced this phrase into the Western linguistic bloodstream. Johann Sebastian Bach and George Frideric Handel used to write this Latin term—SDG—at the end of their compositions.[4] This detail is no mere factoid; it is in human terms a marvelous key to unlocking this doctrine. Every believer, whether in formal ministry or not, may live unto God for the purpose of magnifying His greatness. God was the reason composers composed and musicians played. We give Him glory by a full-orbed Christian life, whatever our precise role in the kingdom may be.[5]

In what follows, we delve into Scripture to understand the biblical idea of "glory." Following this, we survey how the Reformers understood the role of divine glory in the Christian life. We conclude by suggesting four ways that Christians today may live for God's glory alone.

MAN GLORIFYING GOD:
THE POINT OF EVERYTHING

The point of everything in the Christian life, as Paul relays it, is derived from a most unexpected place: a lengthy discussion of food laws. In 1 Corinthians 10, the apostle strives to help a young body of believers, living in a pagan context marked by idol worship and food sacrifices to false gods, understand what to eat and what not to eat.

The apostle gives his confused followers numerous helpful points about how to handle food consecrated in the name of idols. If food is served in these terms, the wise Christian will avoid giving offense to less-mature believers, but he will also feel free to eat such food among unbelievers with the understanding—at a personal level—that false gods do not exist and that the food on the plate is just that: tasty particles. Concluding this section, Paul gives these memorable words: "So, whether you eat or drink, or whatever you do, do all to the glory of God" (v. 31).[6] Through his apostle, God slips the very purpose of existence—and the heartbeat of Christian faith—into a discussion of dietary practices.[7]

Whatever you do. It's not just your particular approach to idolatrous food that gives you a platform by which to glorify God. The Christ follower approaches every single moment of existence as an opportunity to magnify God.[8] You can do this in eating, drinking, reading philosophy, assembling a chair, listening to someone talk during a conversation, playing basketball, performing a bypass, printing T-shirts, praising Christ, making beautiful music, apologizing to a friend you have wronged, playing dolls with your daughter, laughing with your wife, and ten thousand other God-glorifying endeavors of the Christian life. *Whatever you do.*[9]

This matters for making decisions. The common way you and I approach decision making is this: we try to discern, through prayer and counsel and Bible-reading, what the God-glorifying pathway is. I in no way demean such an undertaking. These are exactly the right practices when confronted with opportunities. But we may add a component to our process, one that matters greatly. Paul's focus in this section is on the heart-attitude of the

Christian. He's effectively saying to believers, "Do what honors God. Do what pleases him. Don't do what dishonors him." We can tie ourselves in knots trying to parse how to honor our King when our King has already expressly told us how to live.[10]

We see that God is keenly interested in us, and we should be keenly interested in Him. We do *all* to the glory of God.[11] We are the children of our heavenly Father, adopted into His family through the redemptive work of His Son, and bearing the fruit of holiness through the power of the indwelling Spirit. Like a loving, trusting child in a happy home, we continually seek—from a heart of thankfulness and joy—to honor the family name.[12] Our life is not a fretful one in which we fear to take a step of faith lest we get struck down where we stand. The God-glorifying life is the free life, the joyful existence, and it looks like an all-out pursuit of magnifying the excellency of the Divine.[13]

This is what *soli Deo gloria* boils down to: an existence that savors of God. To better understand just how different such a life is from a non-Christian one, we should go back thousands of years and think about the conflict that ruined this world. To grasp the God-glorifying life versus the man-glorifying one, we travel back in time to Eden.

GOD VERSUS MAN: THE FUNDAMENTAL CONFLICT OVER GLORY

The Bible is not a spiritual self-help book. It's not merely a collection of timeless wisdom. It's not a theological fantasy work, replete with separated seas and fire-breathing dragons and Leviathan. The Bible is at base a true story of a death-struggle between sworn enemies: God and Satan. Both of these figures want glory, but only one of them—God—deserves it. Though the details of the origins of this terrible conflict are shrouded in mystery, it seems that Satan sought to seize the majestic place of God, hungering after His authority, power, and renown (see Luke 10:18; Isa. 14:12). The Lord cast Satan out of His heavenly court for doing so, setting the stage for Genesis 3, where the anti-God tempts Adam and Eve to emulate him, disobey the Lord's command, and set themselves up as their own authority.[14] As we know, the first couple make a terrible choice, and mankind falls as a result. The race made for eternal glory now deserves eternal judgment for sin.[15]

Though the Lord could have shut the whole enterprise down at this point, He did not. He laid out the next stage of battle in the great war of the cosmos in Genesis 3:15, promising the serpent—Satan—that he would bruise the heel of the woman's offspring, but that this same figure would crush the serpent's head.[16] From this inspiring promise, the rest of history was set in motion, and the conflict between God and the devil was fully framed. This conflict, as is by now clear, is a conflict of glory. God is identified in Genesis 1–2 as the Creator of all things. By rights, He possesses lordship and sovereignty over all things. Satan, by contrast, creates nothing; Satan is the rightful lord and sovereign of no one. But this truth does not stop Satan from despising the glory of God and coveting it with deadly force.[17]

This matters for us because, from birth, we do not follow the true King, but the anti-King. We inherit Adam's sin nature, every last one of us. No one teaches us to sin; we do not go to a special pre-kindergarten degree program to hone our lying, aggression against others, and fruit-snacks-stealing abilities. We do these things *naturally*, literally from our Adam-inherited nature (see Rom. 3:10–18; 5:12–21; 1 Cor. 15). But here is the deeper reality: we do not merely do wrong things. We commit sinful acts—or fail to do what we should—because *our heart seeks its own glory*.[18] At an innate level, fallen mankind doesn't want God to be God. We don't want the Lord to get the glory that is due His name. We want glory for ourselves. Remember what John the Baptist said when Christ began His earthly ministry? "He must increase, but I must decrease" (John 3:30). That is the opposite of what we desire as sinners. *I must increase, and all others—including God Himself—must decrease.*[19]

You can find this instinct all over the Bible. Sadly, it pops up among the people of God just as it does among unbelievers. The tower of Babel, for example, is a foolish attempt to assert human power and genius in the face of God (Gen. 11). David numbering Israel shows profound pride, as does his son Solomon giving a tour of all his wealth (1 Chron. 21; 1 Kings 10). Nebuchadnezzar voices the self-glory that surges through the wicked heart, reminding everyone around him of his personal awesomeness: "Is not this great Babylon, which I have built," he roars from the roof of his palace (Dan. 4:30). Wicked Herod so wishes to cling to his power that he strikes down a generation of infant boys whom he fears will usurp his position (Matt. 2). The religious leaders of Jesus' day do not fall on their faces when He teaches them with holy authority, but they oppose Him, blaspheme Him, and ultimately send Him to His death. The beast of Revelation seeks to devour the child of God and overturn the very plan of the divine (Rev. 12). Over and again in the story of Scripture, human pride strives and connives to obscure the glory of God. But this awful effort has never worked. In truth, it never will.[20]

We need to understand that this is personal. This battle over glory—God's or anyone else's—is not far-off from us. It takes place every moment of our lives. Even the born-again believer must struggle against the natural human instinct for self-glorification.[21] We can pray what John stated—*I must decrease, Lord, and You must increase*—through the Spirit's power. But we will have to give effort to actualize this hope. It is not easy to decrease. The desire to increase in prominence and influence and fame and power, by contrast, comes easily to us, even those of us who know Christ. The "glory battle" is not just *out there*. It is *in here*, in our hearts and minds.

When the church confesses *soli Deo gloria*, then, we are not using the watchword of a bygone era. We are calling ourselves and all the children of God to die to self and live to Christ. This is serious business. There may be times when we say "SDG!" with a heart, singing with happiness. There will surely be other times when we whisper this great Reformational slogan with our teeth clenched. We must wage war, spiritual war, if we will amplify the beauty and greatness of God. The true Christian walk is no stroll through the tulips; it is a conflict, a quest, a fight for faith.

A DISTINCTLY SPIRITUAL EXISTENCE: THE DIFFERENCES BETWEEN COMPETING VISIONS OF GLORY

Christians are not the only group in history to formulate a vision of the glorious life, however. As we have been at pains to say, our hearts are naturally glory-hungry. Few societies have focused more on the pursuit of personal greatness more than ancient Greece, making Christianity a direct competitor of several noteworthy movements.

For the Spartans, personal renown—and communal pride— accrued through rugged, heroic, fearless courage in battle. The Spartans trained their soldiers not to fear death, but instead to pursue *kleos* (glory) through great deeds and even a fearless death.[22] The Athenians prized wisdom and erudition. They produced great philosophers, writers, and poets, and gained a reputation as learned and wise. They sought to live out the good life, a life of virtue, and cultivated the intellect, believing that wisdom was an end unto itself. The Epicureans were even more focused on pleasure than the previous groups. They sought the glory of the indulgent existence. Those who deserved honor were those who gorged on pleasure, who refused to let silly moral or religious constraints slow them down in their quest for fleshly delight.[23]

The Christian vision of glory—and the glory-captivated pilgrimage—includes elements of these ideas. Put differently, the natural man can recognize the goodness of the created order, but cannot see the world as God's Word depicts it, and so cannot put together a truly virtuous, righteous, God-honoring life. The Spartans were right to esteem courage and to oppose evil to the full. The Athenians rightly saw how enjoyable and profitable the pursuit of wisdom is. The Epicureans correctly understood that pleasure-seeking is an essential part of a truly happy life. But without Christ, all this thinking fell flat. Christ is the key to a proper vision of glory. Christ was courageous and crushed the head of Satan on the cross. Christ is the very *Logos* of God; He is wisdom. Christ is the pathway to both righteousness and true pleasure (Ps. 16:11). Everything else is counterfeit.[24]

Give us Christ, and we can make sense of these different visions of the glorious existence. God, it turns out, is not in the business of squelching the human interest in grandness, greatness, and honor. God is in the business of re-routing this interest, redeeming it, and sending it heavenward. The Lord wants to take self-centered glory-seekers and make them God-centered glory-seekers. He does not want His true disciples to exchange a vibrant life for a grim but godly sojourn. He wants His church to embrace a glory-seeking life filled with courage, mortification of the flesh, wisdom, holiness, truth, and Godward pleasure. Coming to faith in Christ does not mean shutting one's mind down and numbly going through the spiritual motions. It means taking holistic dominion of the world, and orienting one's intellect, heart, passion, spirituality, ethics, and soul toward God.[25]

The Protestant Reformers understood this. Calvin famously pictured the whole universe as "the theater of God's glory," viewing life as an exhilarating theistic performance before God.[26] All history, and all our lives, are part of a great drama that unfolds with every breath we take. Luther saw glory in the quiet, mundane aspects of the day and memorably cited the changing of diapers as an activity that pleased God:

> Now you tell me, when a father goes ahead and washes
> diapers or performs some other mean task for his
> child, and someone ridicules him as an effeminate fool,
> though that father is acting in the spirit just described
> and in Christian faith, my dear fellow you tell me,
> which of the two is most keenly ridiculing the other?
> God, with all his angels and creatures, is smiling, not
> because that father is washing diapers, but because he is
> doing so in Christian faith.[27]

In their return to Scripture, the Reformers recovered the simple beauty and honorable nature of an ordinary Christian walk. They are sometimes known as theologians who advocated lofty formulations and hard-to-understand ideas. But, in truth, the Reformers recovered the heart of the Christian faith.

It is no surprise that the Reformation vision of glory

catalyzed many in that era. The Reformation helped birth thriving economies and vigorous markets in the sixteenth-century. The Dutch, who embraced Reformational ideas early on, became legendary for their enterprising nature (married to a scrupulous ethical code). Luther's teaching galvanized not only young seminarians, but artists and musicians and politicians. Instead of seeing Christianity in terms of what priests did, the Reformers saw Christianity as a venture in which every believer worked *coram Deo*—in the presence of God. Everyone has a "calling," not only ministry leaders. Everyone is to glorify God as they live to make His name great. The Reformation recovered the biblical truth that doxology (glorifying God) is the motivation of not only the pastor, but the craftsman, the father, the mother, and the quiet and anonymous Christian seeking to obey God by the power of Christ.[28]

Derived from the Word, the Reformation doctrine of *soli Deo gloria* enchants everyday life. But it also warns us. In his writing and teaching, Luther introduced a helpful distinction. He distinguished "theologians of glory" from "theologians of the cross."[29] In his mind, theologians of glory seek power from God. They want to be great, known, and strong. They do not come to Christ to die and decrease, but to draw power from on high and increase among men.[30] In doing so, theologians of glory seek God apart from Christ. For Luther, Philip exhibited this tendency of the *theologia gloriae* ("theology of glory"): "Philip said to him, 'Lord, show us the Father, and it is enough for us'"

(John 14:8). In this instance, Philip did not wish to follow the Christ who was on His way to Calvary. He wanted the Father, the power, the glory. He did not see that the Father had sent the Son, and that the only way to the Father was thus through the Son. The narrow way that the Son was walking, a way that led unto death, was the same narrow way that all His followers would have to tread.

Sharp-eyed readers are seeing at this point that "best life now" theology is not new, but ancient.[31] Like Simon the magician, people are happy to follow God or His Son if they sense that He will upgrade their lives, smooth out their troubles, and bless them as they deserve. We often hear that ours is a secular age, and in some ways—at elite levels in particular—it may be, but it is actually quite spiritual.[32] But here we must ask: *Which spirituality are people interested in. And if they are interested in Jesus, which Jesus? The Jesus of Americana or the Christ of Faith?* If we are not careful, we may follow God not because of genuine love for Him but due to our instinctive hunger for health, self-improvement, balance, and greatness. If we do not watch ourselves, we can slip into the all-too-common trap, and make Jesus a wellness plan, a self-improvement scheme, a get-rich-quick method. If Luther is to be believed, and the theology of glory is a real temptation, we must make sure that the Christ we are following is the biblical Christ.

For Luther, Christ's cross is everything, so he said, "The cross alone is our theology" (*crux sola est nostra theologia*).[33] His theology of the cross is the opposite of the theology of glory. If we would truly know Christ, we must know His crucifixion. We must find Him in His hour of suffering. We must find peace with our God through Christ's bloody atonement. Then, when we are made new spiritually through repentance and faith, we must take up our own cross, and follow Him. It may well be the case that doing so invites suffering, persecution, and even death. But whatever the cost we each face for our faith is all worth it, for we will go to Christ immediately upon our death, we will live in heaven with Him, and we will reign with Him in all eternity in the New Jerusalem.

One additional point demands articulation. Many good-hearted Christians would affirm what Luther called "the theology of the cross." They would think that they should be ready for suffering and trials if they come. This is a good instinct, but it does not do full justice to the scriptural teaching on suffering in the Christian life. When we trust Christ as Savior, we enter the way of suffering. It is not, in other words, that suffering *could* visit us; it is that suffering surely *will* visit us. In coming to faith in Jesus, we place a target on our back right alongside the heavy, splintered cross we have taken up.[34] But as hard as it can be to see in the moment, even our suffering is not outside the will of God and is not able to keep us from glorifying God despite our weakness. Our weakness, in fact, only magnifies the Lord's mercy and grace all the more, especially when we bear it with a Christ-centered outlook.

Every Christian is a participant in the pageant of pain. We "share abundantly in Christ's sufferings" (2 Cor. 1:5). We cannot be "surprised at the fiery trial when it comes" upon us (1 Peter 4:12). We share in Christ's sufferings in order that we would share in His glory (Rom. 8:17). Again, it is not that we *might* someday go through a challenge; it is that we have *surely* joined with Christ in His travail. We must not thus panic or blame God when trials come. Instead, we must remember that this is the shape of Christianity in a sin-plagued world, and that our suffering will yield an eternal weight of glory (2 Cor. 4:17). What a help this is to us. The Christ we worship is so glorious that even suffering cannot stop us from magnifying the greatness of the one who saved us.

FOUR IMPLICATIONS
OF THE GOD-GLORIFYING LIFE

As we have seen, *soli Deo gloria*—which signifies living for God's glory alone—is an explosive little phrase. It sums up the very purpose of the cosmos and the driving concern of the Christian life. We must ask, though: "What does this phrase—and mindset—mean at a practical level?" Here are four takeaways from our biblical, theological, and historical survey that can focus our doxological efforts.

First, the glory of God infuses every Christian's life with meaning. We are actors in the drama of redemption. Do not misunderstand: We do not have a starring role. That is Christ's, by the plan and direction of God the Father, and through the agency of God the Spirit. And yet God has chosen to bring us into the show. As we have said, the Lord in His kindness takes us who are naturally self-oriented glory-seekers and makes us God-centered glory-seekers. This means that every believer—the musician like Bach, the theologian like Melanchthon, the artist like Luther's friend Lucas Cranach—may glorify their God on a daily, hourly, basis.[35]

Second, the glory of God is uniquely displayed in Bible-preaching churches. Jesus, the very embodiment of glory, did not establish just any organization during His time on earth. He formed one and only one institution from His blood and by His Father's design: the church (Matt. 16). The church, composed of all His blood-bought followers, is called to be an embassy of heaven in a sin-ravaged world. Every local church serves as a point of heavenly light, no matter the size, no matter the culture's opinion of it.[36] While we have time, let us give great energy and attention to strengthening our local church, whatever our role in it. Doing so defies Satan and honors the Lord who will power His church to overcome the restless evil that seeks to undo it.

If we would have churches that throb and pulse with divine glory, we need biblical-centrality. The Word, after all, is the Spirit-powered instrument and cornerstone of spiritual growth (2 Tim. 3:16). God has called His church to train up elders to provide theological leadership and spiritual oversight of His local congregations (1 Tim. 2–3; Titus 1). If we want our churches to be healthy, we need to raise up godly men who will—under the congregation's authority—shepherd the flock and preach the Word.[37] As in the days of the Reformation, sound doctrine from the pulpit will produce sound living in the pew, which will reap a harvest of glory for the Lord.

Third, the glory of God is connected to holiness. God is chiefly honored and shown to be great by holiness, conformity to His character. This is important to understand: Living a doxological life is not fundamentally about being as cultural, and thus as contextually normal, as we possibly can be. It is primarily about being as godly as we can be through the power of Christ in us. This happens when we lovingly trust that God has saved us to transform us, and we commit ourselves to regular Bible reading, prayer, godly service, and our church. It's not that our works save us; it's that our works display the faith that has taken root in our heart. Pursuing holiness in a serious, even lazer-focused way, is not "legalistic"; it's the very definition of a grace-driven walk with Christ. Grace, after all, is not weak, but strong, stronger than Satan and all his armies.[38]

Fourth, the glory of God reminds us of the beginning and end of all things. *Soli Deo gloria* is a phrase that points us back to God. He is the one who made all things (in creation). He is the one who will remake all things (when eternity dawns). He is the ground of reality. He is beauty and grace and holiness. At the end of the day, our lives are always going to involve some measure of confusion, pain, sadness, and struggle. We find happiness and peace in a fallen world by lifting our eyes to the hills. God is real. God is good. God is in the process of increasing, even as we are decreasing. We are becoming holy; God is getting glory.

We began with the story of Eric Liddell. Many have felt warmed by his inspirational running story as depicted in *Chariots of Fire*. But they don't know how his life ended. As noted in the introduction, Liddell moved to China to undertake missions work. He worked hard for several years to make Christ known among the Chinese until the Japanese war machine pushed into his region. Just before this happened, Liddell sent his wife and young children away to safety in Canada, never to see them again. Not long after, he was placed in a Japanese prison camp. There, in a tiny enclosure alongside nearly 2,000 other people, Liddell still acted as a Christian witness. In a desperate place, he acted kindly, interacted with others cheerfully, and conducted himself morally.[39]

There was a Russian prostitute in the camp, one whom many men would help—but only for a price. According to her years later, they "demanded favors" from her in exchange for assistance. There was only one exception to this rule: Eric Liddell. He built shelves for her, and was gracious to her in conversation, and asked nothing from her.[40]

Not long after this, Liddell grew sick. Suffering from a brain tumor, he died in 1945, not long before the end of the war. In his last days, there were no crowds to cheer him, no papers to cover his brutal physical pain, no grains of sand on which to run mile after mile. No wonder *Chariots of Fire* did not tell this story, for outside of the eyes of faith, it is a story the unbelieving heart cannot understand. Why give it all up? Why die early in life? Why not seize every enviable prize this world could give?

The answer was as simple for Liddell as it was for Christ, for the early church martyrs, for Huss, for Wycliffe, for Luther, for Calvin, for the slain Anabaptists, and for a host of others, too many to count, all of whom will gather in the new heavens and new earth:

For the glory of God alone.

CONCLUSION

While the Reformation began over 500 years ago, the five *solas* ought to be intentionally integrated into every evangelical church's life and ministry today. The five *solas*, as you have seen, represent not only the core of the Protestant Reformation, but also the essential aspects of New Testament Christianity and Great Commission witness. If the church neglects the five *solas*, it does so to its own peril.

Taken together, the fives *solas* are not like a precious crown merely to be observed and appreciated. They are more like concrete, forming the foundation of the church and the support structure for its pulpit and discipleship ministries. What is more, the *solas* of the Reformation are also life-giving for the individual believer. *Sola Scriptura* teaches us that God's Word, and God's Word alone, is our final authority. Thus, we return to the Word again and again for instruction, which forms our beliefs and practices.

Sola gratia teaches us that we must depend on the finished work of Christ alone. We are called to good deeds as those who are found in Christ. We do not undertake such works with hopes of solidifying our salvation or strengthening our assurance. We are saved by God's grace alone, not by our merit.

Similarly, justification *sola fide* is a direct repudiation of the excesses of the Roman Catholic Church, both then and now. *Sola fide* reminds us of the great chasm between Protestant Christianity and the official teachings of Rome. To be sure, as Martin Luther taught us, we are justified by faith alone, but justifying faith is never alone. The fact that we are justified by faith alone is indeed a truth upon which the church stands or falls.

Additionally, *solus Christus* is the ground of our salvation. As believers, we preach a gospel that calls all people to place their faith specifically, exclusively in Jesus Christ alone for salvation. This great truth makes Christianity a singular religion. True believers are those who have, in the words of Christ, found Him to be the way, the truth, and the life, and who believe that no man can come to the Father but through Him (John 14:6).

All the *solas* beautifully roll up together in an ongoing testimony *soli Deo gloria* through the redemptive work of Christ and in the lives of the redeemed. Thus, salvation unto God's glory alone is a reminder of why God has performed His great, redeeming work through His Son, Jesus Christ, and why He chose to grant salvation to His people—for His great glory. Thus, our lives as believers are to be lived with the ambition of giving Him greater glory, and we are to likewise read our Bibles and engage in the life of the church, which is the prism of God's own glory.

Thus, these five great truths, the *solas* of the Reformation, are perennial, enduring truths. We are not to limit our reflection on the five *solas* to periodic celebrations of the Protestant Reformation, but we are to see them as perpetually essential convictions. They serve as the theological superstructure for evangelical Christianity and as the great signposts of our Christian lives.

Five hundred years ago, God raised up key men, especially Martin Luther, to trumpet anew the gospel of grace. In our generation, may we be part of a great cadre of men and women who likewise trumpet God's grace as articulated through the *solas* of the Reformation. Indeed, the former's cry must be ours as well. We are to labor for a church reformed and always reforming.

ACKNOWLEDGMENTS

To varying degrees, every book takes a number of talented and dedicated individuals to bring it to fruition—it is especially true with this one. First, I am grateful for my colleagues—Jason Duesing, Owen Strachan, Matthew Barrett, and Jared Wilson—who chose to join in this project. I value these men as good friends, gifted leaders and teachers, faithful ministers of the gospel, and accomplished scholars. They not only made this book better, but made it possible.

At the personal level, God has abundantly blessed me with a wife in Karen, and a family in Anne-Marie, Caroline, William, Alden, and Elizabeth, who have surpassed my every hope and dream as to what they'd be and mean to me. They provide as much love, joy, support, and satisfaction as I could have ever imagined. Without them, my life and ministry would not be nearly as fulfilling.

At the institutional level, my colleagues and office staff likewise are an invaluable source of support and encouragement. Most especially, I'm thankful for Patrick Hudson, Tyler Sykora,

Catherine Crouse, and Dawn Philbrick. These men and women serve our Lord Jesus and Midwestern Seminary well and faithfully. Daily, they encourage and inspire me with their kindness and competence as they carry out their many responsibilities. It brings me great joy to serve with them.

Furthermore, I'm thankful to the team at Moody Publishers, most especially Kevin Emmert and Drew Dyck. These men have provided invaluable insight throughout the project and, along with the publisher they serve, make great partners.

Lastly, and most of all, I'm indebted to my Lord and Savior, Jesus Christ. Without His grace, calling, and gifting, my actions would be insufficient. It is only by Him and through Him that I can accomplish anything in this life. May He receive all the glory for any fruit that results from this book.

NOTES

Chapter 1: Scripture Alone

1. Martin Luther, *Three Treatises* (Philadelphia: Fortress Press, 1998), 238.
2. See Jason K. Allen, *Discerning Your Call to Ministry: How to Know for Sure and What to Do About It* (Chicago: Moody Publishers, 2016), 22.
3. Steven J. Lawson, "Fortress for Truth: Martin Luther" as found at https://www.ligonier.org/blog/fortress-truth-martin-luther/.
4. Derek Wilson, *Out of the Storm: The Life and Legacy of Martin Luther* (New York: St. Martin's Press, 2007), 123.
5. Aaron Denlinger, "The Goose," as found at https://www.ligonier.org/learn/articles/goose/. The Surname "Hus," derived from Hus's place of birth Husinec, means "goose" in Czech.

Chapter 2: Grace Alone

1. Martin Luther, *A Commentary on Saint Paul's Epistle to the Galatians* (London: James Duncan, 1830), 1–2.
2. Kevin J. Vanhoozer, *Biblical Authority after Babel: Retrieving the Solas in the Spirit of Mere Protestant Christianity* (Grand Rapids: Brazos, 2016), 64.
3. "Antinomianism" basically means "against the law" and refers to the false teaching that those who are saved by grace are free to disobey the moral law of God.
4. John Calvin, *Institutes of the Christian Religion*, ed. John T. McNeill, trans. Ford Lewis Battles (Philadelphia: Westminster John Knox Press, 1960), 3.11.7.
5. Ibid.
6. J. Gresham Machen, *Christianity and Liberalism* (Grand Rapids: Wm. B. Eerdmans Publishing Co., 2009), 21.
7. Martin Luther, *A Commentary on St. Paul's Epistle to the Galatians*, trans. Theodore Graebner (Christian Classics Ethereal Library, n.d.), n.p., https://www.ccel.org/ccel/luther/galatians.

8. Nathan W. Bingham, "By Grace Alone: An Interview with Sinclair Ferguson," Ligonier Ministries, June 6, 2014, http://www.ligonier.org/blog/grace-alone-interview-sinclair-ferguson/.

9. Philip Paul Bliss, "Free from the law, o happy condition" (1871).

Chapter 3: Faith Alone

1. C. S. Lewis, *The Silver Chair* (New York: MacMillan, 1953).

2. See Jeffrey P. Greenman and Timothy Larsen, eds. *Reading Romans Through the Centuries* (Grand Rapids: Brazos Press, 2005).

3. Roger Scruton, *Beauty: A Very Short Introduction* (Oxford: Oxford University Press, 2011), 3–4.

4. Martyn Lloyd-Jones, *Romans: An Exposition of Chapter 1* (Edinburgh: Banner of Truth, 1985), 278.

5. Lloyd-Jones, *Romans*, 308.

6. Roland Bainton, *Here I Stand: A Life of Martin Luther* (Peabody, MA: Hendrickson, 2011), 1.

7. Justo L. Gonzalez, *A History of Christian Thought*, vol. III (Nashville: Abingdon, 1987), 30.

8. Ibid., 31.

9. Ibid., 32.

10. *Sermons I in Luther's Works* (*LW*), 51:77–78, ed. and trans. John W. Doberstein (Minneapolis: Fortress Press, 1959).

11. Martin Luther, "Preface to the Epistle of St. Paul to the Romans" (1522, Revised 1546) in Timothy F. Lull and William R. Russell, eds., *Martin Luther's Basic Theological Writings*, 3rd ed. (Minneapolis: Fortress Press, 2012), 76; *Word and Sacrament I* in *Luther's Works* (*LW*), 35:365, ed. and trans. E. Theodore Bachman (Minneapolis: Fortress Press, 1960).

12. Martin Luther, "Preface to the Complete Edition Luther's Latin Writings" (1545), in Lull and Russell, eds., *Martin Luther's Basic Theological Writings*, 496–97; *LW* 34:336–38.

13. See Tom Schreiner's evaluation of the New Perspective on Paul in *Faith Alone: The Doctrine of Justification* (Grand Rapids,: Zondervan, 2015), 239–261.

14. "Justification," in Timothy George and Thomas G. Guarino, eds., *Evangelicals and Catholics Together at Twenty* (Ada, MI: Brazos, 2015), 24–37.

15. The Lutheran World Federation and the Roman Catholic Church, *Joint Declaration on the Doctrine of Justification* (Grand Rapids: Wm. B. Eerdmans Publishing Co., 2000).

16. See Michael Horton, "Prologue: What Are We Celebrating?" in Matthew Barrett, ed., *Reformation Theology* (Wheaton, IL: Crossway, 2017), 20–34.

17. Ibid., 21.

18. For a further helpful discussion of the relationship of Roman Catholicism to Protestantism, see R. C. Sproul, *Are We Together? A Protestant Analyzes*

Roman Catholicism (Orlando: Reformation Trust, 2012).

19. Clyde Kilby, "Eleven Resolutions to Guide Life," in *The Arts and the Christian Imagination* (Brewster, MA: Paraclete Press, 2016), xvi.

20. As Jonathan Leeman, "A Traditional Protestant Formulation of *Sola Fide* as the Source of Political Unity," in *JBTS* 2.1 (2017): 30, says, "Subjectively, *sola fide* requires an individual 'to reach the end' of him or herself, and his or her self-justifying arguments for self-enthronement. This broken and regretful self therefore asks for a free gift of righteousness, yields the throne once more to God, and embraces those who were once enemies but are now fellow citizens."

Chapter 4: Christ Alone

1. Quoted in Douglas Bond, *Augustus Toplady* (Darlington, England: EP Books), 94.

2. For the whole story, see Roland H. Bainton, *Here I Stand: A Life of Martin Luther* (Peabody, MA: Hendrickson, 1950; 2012), 14–15.

3. To see Luther's mature understanding of Christ alone, see his *Lectures on Galatians, 1535,* in *Luther's Works*, American Edition, 55 vols., eds. Jaroslav Pelikan and Helmut T. Lehmann (Philadelphia: Muehlenberg and Fortress, and St. Louis: Concordia, 1955–1986), vol. 26.

4. For a more involved answer to this question, see Matthew Barrett, "Can This Bird Fly? Repositioning the Genesis of the Reformation on Martin Luther's Early Polemic against Gabriel Biel's Covenantal, Voluntarist Doctrine of Justification," *The Southern Baptist Journal of Theology* 21, no. 4 (2017): 61–102.

5. *Catechism of the Catholic Church* (New York: Doubleday, 1995), section 1584. Cf. Stephen Wellum, *Christ Alone: The Uniqueness of Jesus as Savior* (Grand Rapids: Zondervan, 2017), 262.

6. For Rome there are seven: baptism, the Eucharist, penance, confirmation, marriage, ordination, and extreme unction.

7. For Luther's response, see *The Babylonian Captivity of the Church, 1520,* in *LW* 36:3–126.

8. What Rome called operative power. Richard A. Muller, *Dictionary of Latin and Greek Theological Terms*, 2nd ed. (Grand Rapids: Baker Academic, 2017), 113.

9. This was declared in its seventh session (1547); see canons 5, 6, 8, in Jaroslav Pelikan and Valerie R. Hotchkiss, eds., *Creeds & Confessions of Faith in the Christian Tradition* (New Haven, CT: Yale University Press, 2003), 2:836–37.

10. "The mass is a promise of the forgiveness of sins made to us by God, and such a promise as has been confirmed by the death of the Son of God." Luther, *Babylonian Captivity*, in *LW* 36:38.

11. Luther, *Babylonian Captivity*, in *LW* 36:46–47. For a further explanation, see Alister E. McGrath, *Reformation Thought*, 4th ed. (Oxford: Wiley-Blackwell, 2012), 164.

12. Timothy J. Wengert, *Martin Luther's 95 Theses* (Minneapolis: Fortress Press, 2015), xvi.

13. John Tetzel, "A Sermon [1517]," in Hans J. Hillerbrand, ed., *The Protestant Reformation*, rev. ed. (New York: Harper Perennial, 2009), 19–21. Accompanying these indulgences were thousands of relics from the saints, and if viewed with reverence could also lessen time in purgatory. Churchgoers were taught that they should also pray to these saints, Mary being at the top of that hierarchy, being the mother of Jesus, the one who has Jesus' ear.

14. Luther to Archbishop Albert of Mainz, October 31, 1517, in *LW* 48:46.

15. See John Calvin, *Institutes of the Christian Religion*, ed. John T. McNeill, trans. Ford Lewis Battles (Philadelphia: Westminster John Knox Press, 1960), 3.4.26. Also see Articles XVII and XX in Ulrich Zwingli's "The Sixty-Seven Articles (1523)," in James T. Dennison Jr., ed., *Reformed Confessions of the 16th and 17th Centuries in English Translation* (Grand Rapids: Reformation Heritage Books, 2008), 1:4.

16. Calvin, *Institutes* 2.15.6. cf. 4.18.1–3. Also see Luther, *Babylonian Captivity*, in *LW* 36:50–51.

17. Calvin, *Institutes* 2.16.19.

18. Ibid.

19. "The Heidelberg Catechism (1563)," in James T. Dennison, ed., *Reformed Confessions*, 2:771.

20. Luther, *Babylonian Captivity*, in *LW* 36:57.

Chapter 5: Glory to God Alone

1. See the engrossing and well-reported biography by Duncan Hamilton, *For the Glory: Eric Liddell's Journey from Olympic Champion to Modern Martyr* (New York: Penguin, 2016).

2. For a helpful introduction to Reformation doctrine, see Matthew Barrett, ed., *Reformation Theology: A Systematic Summary* (Wheaton, IL: Crossway, 2017); and the classic resource—and justly so—Timothy George, *Theology of the Reformers* (Nashville: B&H Academic, 2013 [1988]).

3. The exact *provenance* of the *solas* is not known. In the Reformation era, Philip Melanchthon, for example, wrote that "*sola gratia justificamus et sola fide justificamur*" ("only by grace do we justify and only by faith are we justified"). In 1916, Lutheran scholar Theodore Engelder published an article titled "The Three Principles of the Reformation: Sola Scriptura, Sola Gratia, Sola Fides" ("only scripture, only grace, only faith"). Theologian Emil Brunner later added *soli deo gloria* and *Christus solus* to this list. For

further information, see R. Michael Allen, *Reformed Theology* (Continuum International Publishing Group, 2010).

4. In the eighteenth century, Bach wrote "SDG" at the bottom of most of his scores. Handel often used the formulation as well, as on the last page of his magisterial *Messiah*. See Calvin Stapert, "To the Glory of God Alone," *Christian History* 95 (2007), accessible at http://www.christianitytoday. com/history/issues/issue-95/to-glory-of-god-alone.html; Don Samdahl, "Handel's Messiah," *Doctrine.org*, July 2014, accessible at http://doctrine. org/handels-messiah.

5. For more on this point, consult Michael Reeves, *The Unquenchable Flame: Discovering the Heart of the Reformation* (Nashville: B&H Academic, 2010).

6. Mark Taylor, *1 Corinthians*, ed. E. Ray Clendenen, vol. 28, The New American Commentary (Nashville, TN: B&H Publishing Group, 2014), 249–50, notes that "Eating and drinking in the ancient world was the locus of relational interaction where dominant worldviews collided. Paul has articulated a very careful gospel-centered decision-making ethic that can be summed up in the maxim, 'Do it all for the glory of God.'"

7. Not for nothing did Karl Barth, *The Resurrection of the Dead* (Eugene, OR: Wipf & Stock, 2003 [1933]), 38, suggest that this verse was the "goal of this section," the focal point of the larger multi-chapter unit dealing with food sacrificed to idols.

8. So say Roy E. Ciampa and Brian S. Rosner, *The First Letter to the Corinthians*, The Pillar New Testament Commentary (Grand Rapids; Cambridge, U.K.: William B. Eerdmans Publishing Company, 2010), 495–98: "The point is that when the Corinthians think about issues related to food and drink (or any other issue), their overriding concern should not be with the exercise of their own rights and freedom or desires but with the potential implications for God's honor and glory."

9. There is at this point strong theological agreement between this perspective and the Kuyperian understanding of all of the universe being claimed by Christ in His famous shout of "Mine!" See Abraham Kuyper, "Sphere Sovereignty" in *Abraham Kuyper: A Centennial Reader*, ed. James D. Bratt (Grand Rapids: Eerdmans, 1998), 488.

10. This view overlaps with that argued by John A. MacArthur, *Found: God's Will* (Colorado Springs: David C. Cook, 2012 [1977]).

11. David VanDrunen, *God's Glory Alone: The Majestic Heart of Christian Faith and Life—What the Reformers Taught . . . and Why It Still Matters*, The 5 Solas Series, ed. Matthew Barrett (Grand Rapids: Zondervan, 2015), 154, is surely right when he charges that *soli Deo gloria* must be understood first as about God, not first about us and how we live.

12. For a stout theological take on soteriological adoption, see David Garner, *Sons in the Son: The Riches and Reach of Adoption in Christ* (Phillipsburg, NJ: P&R, 2012).

13. My usage of the term "excellency" comes from Jonathan Edwards, who used it to speak of the beautiful conjunction of all God's attributes and perfections. For more on a God-centered existence, see Owen Strachan and Douglas Sweeney, *The Essential Jonathan Edwards: An Introduction to the Life and Teaching of America's Greatest Theologian* (Chicago: Moody, 2018).

14. For a readable exploration of the dynamics and consequences of this fall for men and women, see Owen Strachan and Gavin Peacock, *The Grand Design: Male and Female He Made Them* (Fearn, Ross-shire, UK: Christian Focus, 2016).

15. To better understand how we all fell in Adam, see John Murray, *The Imputation of Adam's Sin* (Phillipsburg, NJ: P&R, 1959).

16. Peter Gentry and Stephen Wellum, *God's Kingdom through God's Covenants*, 258, suggest that this promise, the *protoeuangelion*, "drives the entire storyline of the Bible." See also Tom Schreiner, *Covenant and God's Purpose for the World*, Short Studies in Biblical Theology (Wheaton, IL: Crossway, 2017), 19–29.

17. Satan is the first in a tragically-long line of narcissists. For modern commentary on narcissism, see Christopher Lasch, *The Culture of Narcissism: American Life in an Age of Diminishing Expectations* (New York: W. W. Norton, 1979); also Jean M. Twenge, *Generation Me: Why Today's Young Americans Are More Confident, Assertive, Entitled—and More Miserable Than Ever Before* (New York: Free Press, 2006).

18. Our sin is as much a product of self-idolatry as it is any other factor. Hence, Calvin's famous statement: "From this we may gather that man's nature, so to speak, is a perpetual factory of idols. Man's mind, full as it is of pride and boldness, dares to imagine a god according to its own capacity; as it sluggishly plods, indeed is overwhelmed with the crassest ignorance, it conceives an unreality and an empty appearance as God." John Calvin, *Institutes of the Christian Religion* ed. John T. McNeill, trans. Ford Lewis Battles (Philadelphia: Westminster John Knox, 1960), 1.11.8.

19. At the heart of the doxological impulse is humility. For more here, see C. J. Mahaney, *Humility: True Greatness* (Colorado Springs: Multnomah, 2005).

20. To gain a fuller sense for a biblical theology of glory, consult VanDrunen, *God's Glory Alone*, 43–108.

21. A noteworthy work in this field is Rebecca Konyndyk DeYoung, *Vainglory: The Forgotten Vice* (Grand Rapids: Eerdmans, 2014).

22. Harvey Mansfield, *Manliness* (New Haven, CT: Yale University Press, 2006), offers a thoughtful critique and analysis of ancient warrior culture.

23. For one reference point on an ancient view of glory, see Walter Hamilton, ed., *Plato: The Symposium* (New York: Penguin Classics, 1951).

24. God is the greatest gift of them all. To understand a joyful approach to the Lord—and by extension the world He has made—see John Piper, *Desiring God: Meditations of a Christian Hedonist*, 2nd ed. (Colorado Springs: Multnomah, 2011 [1986]).

25. Books that urge this kind of bold spirit include John Piper, *Risk Is Right: Better to Lose Your Life Than Waste It* (Wheaton, IL: Crossway, 2013); David Platt, *Radical: Taking Your Faith Back from the American Dream* (Colorado Springs: Multnomah, 2010); Owen Strachan, *Risky Gospel: Abandon Fear and Build Something Awesome* (Nashville: Thomas Nelson, 2013).

26. See Calvin, *Institutes*, 1.5.8; 2.6.1.

27. Martin Luther, "The Estate of Marriage" (1522), in *Martin Luther's Basic Theological Writings*, 2nd edition, ed. Timothy F. Lull (Minneapolis: Augsburg Fortress, 2005), 158–59.

28. For a fuller picture of these ideas, see Gene Edward Veith Jr., *God at Work: Your Christian Vocation in All of Life* (Wheaton, IL: Crossway, 2011); Abraham Kuyper, *Lectures on Calvinism* (Peabody, MA: Hendrickson, 2008 [1898]); Hugh Whelchel, "The Day the World Changed: The Reformation 500 Years Later," The Institute for Faith, Work, and Economics, October 31, 2017, https://tifwe.org/the-day-the-world-changed-the-reformation-500-years-later.

29. See VanDrunen, *God's Glory Alone*, 16–18.

30. For more on this gripping concept, see Alister E. McGrath, *Luther's Theology of the Cross: Martin Luther's Theological Breakthrough*, 2nd ed. (Oxford and Malden, MA: Wiley-Blackwell, 2011).

31. I refer here to prosperity theology materials—of either the "hard" or the "soft" version—which should be avoided.

32. While the rise of the "Nones" is real—23 percent in 2015 versus 16 percent in 2007—widespread belief in the afterlife, for example, persists. Most Americans still believe in heaven—72 percent by one count. For more, see Michael Lipka, "A Closer Look at America's Rapidly Growing Religious 'Nones,'" Pew Research Center, May 13, 2015, http://www.pewresearch.org/fact-tank/2015/05/13/a-closer-look-at-americas-rapidly-growing-religious-nones; Carlyle Murphy, "Most Americans Believe in Heaven . . . and Hell," Pew Research Center, November 10, 2015, http://www.pewresearch.org/fact-tank/2015/11/10/most-americans-believe-in-heaven-and-hell; Neil Strauss, "God at the Grammys: The Chosen Ones," *Wall Street Journal*, February 12, 2011, http://online.wsj.com/news/articles/SB10001424052748704858404576134601105583860.

33. Martin Luther, "Lectures on Psalms 1–22," *Weimarer Ausgabe*, 5.176, 32–33. (*WA* stands for the *Weimar* edition of Luther's works in German and Latin.)

34. For more on this topic, see J. Todd Billings, *Rejoicing in Lament: Wrestling with Incurable Cancer and Life in Christ* (Grand Rapids: Brazos Press, 2015).

35. Christians will find a helpful take on honoring God in one's daily life in Michael Horton, *Ordinary: Sustainable Faith in a Radical, Restless World* (Grand Rapids: Zondervan, 2014).

36. For a helpful approach to the local church and its nature, see Mark Dever and Jamie Dunlop, *The Compelling Community: Where God's Power Makes a Church Attractive* (Wheaton, IL: Crossway, 2015).

37. To raise up elders along biblical lines, consult Jeramie Rinne, *Church Elders: How to Shepherd God's People Like Jesus*, 9Marks: Building Healthy Churches (Wheaton, IL: Crossway: 2014).

38. I commend in this endeavor the work of Donald Whitney, *Spiritual Disciplines for the Christian Life* (Colorado Springs: NavPress, 1991).

39. For more details of Liddell's internment, see Barbara Basler, "Chinese Grave's Secret: A Famed Runner Rests Here," *New York Times*, December 2, 1990, http://www.nytimes.com/1990/12/02/world/chinese-grave-s-secret-a-famed-runner-rests-here.html.

40. Hamilton, *For the Glory*, 263.

CONTRIBUTORS

Jason K. Allen (PhD, Southern Baptist Theological Seminary) is President of Midwestern Baptist Theological Seminary and Spurgeon College.

Jared C. Wilson is Director of Content Strategy & Managing Editor of *For the Church* at Midwestern Baptist Theological Seminary.

Jason G. Duesing (PhD, Southeastern Baptist Theological Seminary) is Provost and Associate Professor of Historical Theology at Midwestern Baptist Theological Seminary.

Matthew Barrett (PhD, Southern Baptist Theological Seminary) is Associate Professor of Christian Theology at Midwestern Baptist Theological Seminary.

Owen Strachan (PhD, Trinity Evangelical Divinity School) is Associate Professor of Christian Theology, Director of the Center for Public Theology, and Director of the Residency PhD Program at Midwestern Baptist Theological Seminary.

WHERE WAS THE GOSPEL BEFORE THE REFORMATION?

MOODY Publishers

From the Word to Life

If an evangelical understanding of the gospel is only 500 years old, we are in major trouble. However, if it can be demonstrated that Reformers were not inventing something new, but instead were recovering something old, then key tenets of the Protestant faith are greatly affirmed. Hence, the need for this book.

978-0-8024-1802-9 | also available as an eBook

WHERE WAS THE GOSPEL BEFORE
THE REFORMATION?

A LOT IS EXPECTED OF A PASTOR, BUT WHAT IS ESSENTIAL?

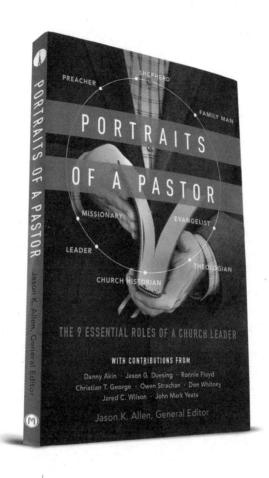

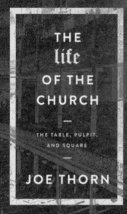

THE **life** | **heart** | **character** OF THE CHURCH

This three-book series is designed for diverse readership. It avoids theological jargon and uses clear terms to keep readers tracking and engaged. Ideal for evangelism and discipleship, each book can be read within an hour and is organized simply for retention. Biblical, balanced, and historically informed, it is useful for Sunday school, one-to-one reading, ministry training, and personal study.

FOR THE
CHURCH

FTC.CO

MOODY
Publishers®

moodypublishers.com

Small ≠ Broken

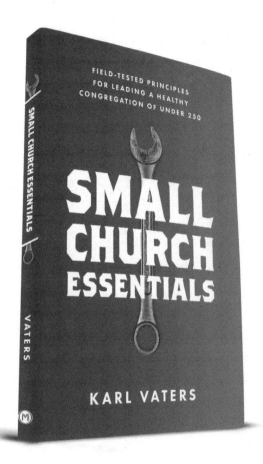